A Geometry of International Trade

First published in 1952, this work is a systematic exposition of Professor Meade's geometric method, bringing together into a single coherent account the modern geometrical analysis of the theory of international trade. The work makes a number of original contributions, notably in the geometrical treatment of domestic production, of the balance of payments, and of import and export duties.

A Geometry of International Trade

J. E. Meade

Routledge
Taylor & Francis Group

First published in 1952 Ltd.
by George Allen & Unwin

This edition first published in 2012 by Routledge
2 Park Square, Milton Park, Abingdon, Oxon, OX14 4RN

Simultaneously published in the USA and Canada
by Routledge
711 Third Avenue, New York, NY 10017

Routledge is an imprint of the Taylor & Francis Group, an informa business

© 1952 George Allen and Unwin Ltd

Publisher's Note
The publisher has gone to great lengths to ensure the quality of this reprint but
points out that some imperfections in the original copies may be apparent.

Disclaimer
The publisher has made every effort to trace copyright holders and welcomes
correspondence from those they have been unable to contact.

A Library of Congress record exists under ISBN: 53000613

ISBN 13: 978-0-415-52630-2 (hbk)
ISBN 13: 978-0-203-10664-8 (ebk)

A GEOMETRY
OF INTERNATIONAL TRADE

James Edward Meade

C.B., M.A.

Professor of Commerce
in the University of London

London

GEORGE ALLEN & UNWIN LTD

Ruskin House   Museum Street

FIRST PUBLISHED IN 1952

PRINTED IN GREAT BRITAIN
in 12-point Baskerville
BY UNWIN BROTHERS LIMITED
WOKING AND LONDON

THIS short book has a limited purpose. It attempts to present systematically the basic technique of the geometry which is often used for the analysis of trade theory. The representations are not used in this book to solve any economic problems. I have elsewhere tried so to use some of them for some purposes, for example in my article "A Geometrical Representation of Balance-of-Payments Policy" in *Economica* for November 1949, reprinted in the Mathematical Supplement to Volume I of my *Theory of International Economic Policy*. But this book is written merely to show how various trade situations may be geometrically represented, so that the student can himself employ the geometrical technique for the solution of the various problems which he subsequently encounters.

To represent international trade in two dimensions naturally demands very great simplification of assumptions. I have tried to lay out these assumptions explicitly in Chapter I of this book. But it is my claim that in some respects rather more can be shown in two dimensions than is often attempted. I was led to develop this technique by attempts to analyse certain fundamental situations in the preparation of my *Theory of International Economic Policy*, which I am preparing under the auspices of the Royal Institute of International Affairs. Often one can hope to obtain some insight into the influence of a particular factor in the complicated real world, in the first place at least, only by isolating its effect in very much simplified circumstances. The result will, of course, give one no more than a "hunch" about the desirability of a particular policy in the real world; for one has to make additional judgments about the effect of further modifications of the over-simplified assumptions. Nevertheless, this method of simple models can, I believe, with care be employed to give useful suggestions about important influences at work in the real world. Accordingly, I appeal to the reader:

Yet sit and see;
Minding true things by what their mockeries be.

Much of what is contained in this book is no more than an attempt to put together systematically the recent work on this subject which has been published in many articles by many authors in many journals. I am much indebted to such papers as: Wassily W. Leontieff, "The Use of Indifferent Curves in the Analysis of Foreign Trade," *Quarterly Journal of Economics*, 1933; A. P. Lerner, "The Symmetry between Import and Export Taxes," *Economica*, 1936; N. Kaldor, "A Note on Tariffs and the Terms of Trade," *Economica*, 1940; Tibor de Scitovszky, "A Reconsideration of the Theory of Tariffs," *Review of Economic Studies*, 1942; A. M. Henderson, "A Geometrical Note on Bulk Purchase," *Economica*, 1948; Lloyd A. Metzler, "Tariffs, the Terms of Trade, and the Distribution of National Income," *Journal of Political Economy*, 1949; R. C. O. Matthews, "Reciprocal Demand and Increasing Returns," *Review of Economic Studies*, 1949–50.

I would like to thank Professor Lionel Robbins and Dr. Helen Makower for reading my MS., and for many helpful comments on it.

J. E. MEADE

LONDON SCHOOL OF ECONOMICS
September 1951

CONTENTS

CHAPTER I

The Assumptions

IN the following representations many of the most severe simplifying assumptions which are normally made in the geometrical analysis of trade theory will be maintained. I shall assume throughout this book:—

(i) that there are only two countries, which we will call country A and country B;

(ii) that there are only two products, which we will call A-exportables and B-exportables. A-exportables are, of course, B-importables, and vice versa;

(iii) that there is perfect competition with no external economies or diseconomies;

(iv) that price flexibility of one kind or another leads to the full employment of resources;

(v) that each country is made up of a set of citizens with identical tastes and factor endowments, so that the indifference map, while it may differ as between a citizen of A and a citizen of B, is the same for all the citizens in either of the two countries. In these conditions we can derive community-indifference curves directly from individual-indifference curves;*

(vi) that the individual's indifference curves are

---

* This strict assumption is necessary if we wish to use the community indifference curves to measure the economic welfare of the community. But, as Mr. Turvey has pointed out to me, if we are concerned only with the determination of the market equilibrium (i.e. of the prices, outputs, and trade in the two commodities) we can be satisfied with the less strict assumption that the relative prices of the two commodities in either country depends only on the total amounts of the two commodities available on the market for consumption in that country, no matter how income is distributed between the citizens of the country. We can then replace the commodity indifference curves by market behaviour curves, of which there will be a unique set independent of the distribution of income. But we can no longer say that the community is necessarily better off if it moves from a lower to a higher market behaviour curve, since the change may have involved an undesirable redistribution of income.

(*a*) negatively sloped (i.e. that an increase in the one commodity is required to compensate for a decrease in the other) and (*b*) convex (i.e. that the more a consumer has of the one commodity on any given indifference curve the greater is the increment in it which is required in order to compensate for a given decrement in the other). We shall also normally assume that neither of the two commodities is an "inferior" good in consumption (i.e. that when a consumer's income increases he purchases more of both commodities or, at least, does not purchase less of either of them); and

(vii) that in both of the two countries the total supply of productive factors is fixed so that when the production of one commodity is increased that of the other must be decreased. In addition we shall normally assume increasing costs, i.e. that the greater is the production of the one commodity the greater is the amount of the other which must be sacrificed in order to produce a still further increment of the first commodity; but in Chapters IV and V respectively we shall digress in order to say something about the geometrical representation of constant costs and of decreasing costs.

The simplifying assumptions which are frequently made in the geometrical representation of the theory of international trade, but which it is our intention to drop in the course of this analysis, are:—

(i) that each country can produce only one of the products. As has already been implied in (vii) above, we shall in fact be assuming throughout this book that each country can produce both commodities, and that there is in each country a production opportunity relationship between the two products of the type outlined in (vii) above;

(ii) that the balance of trade is zero. The purpose of one section of this book will be to show how a balance-of-trade surplus or deficit can be represented geometrically; and

(iii) that the government of a country which receives a revenue from any import or export duty arbitrarily decides whether to spend the revenue on home-produced products (exportables) or foreign-produced products (importables). Another main purpose of this book will be to show how the effect of import and export taxes (or subsidies) can be represented when the indifference map of the citizens is itself allowed to determine the way in which the receipt of additional revenue (or the burden of additional State expenditure) affects the demand for exportable and importable commodities.

CHAPTER II

The Consumption-Indifference Map and the Trade-Indifference Map

CONSIDER first the geometric representation given in Figure I. Measure up the axis OY the amount of B-exportables (or A-importables) consumed in country A and along the axis OX′ (i.e. to the left of O) the amount of A-exportables (or B-importables) consumed in country A. Then in the quadrant X′OY we can draw a map of the A-consumption-indifference curves of which I_c is a representative. Let the block OP′PP″ represent the production possibilities in country A, so that on the assumption of full employment and technically efficient production in A, production in A will be represented by a combination of outputs lying on the line P′PP″. In the closed economy OR of A-exportables and OU of B-exportables will be produced and consumed in country A.

Now let the block OP′PP″ slide up the indifference curve I_c in such a way that the curve P′PP″ remains tangential to I_c and the line P′O remains in a horizontal position. The corner of the block will now trace out the line I_t, Q and Q′ showing two successive positions of the corner with S and T showing the corresponding points of tangency with I_c. We shall call the line I_t the A-trade-indifference curve which corresponds to the A-consumption-indifference curve, I_c.

There will be a trade-indifference curve corresponding to every consumption-indifference curve. The reader must imagine the A-production block OP′PP″ being picked up and placed tangentially against an A-consumption-indifference curve lower than I_c, and then being slid along this lower I_c-curve. A new I_t-curve such as I_t^1 will be traced which will be consistently below the old I_t curve, and which will therefore cut the line OX to the right of O. Similarly the I_t-curve, I_t^2, corresponding to a higher I_c-curve such as I_c^2 will lie consistently above the curve marked I_t and will cut the OY axis above O.

We may now enumerate some of the most important properties of the trade-indifference curves :—

(i) The slope of a trade-indifference curve at any point is equal to the slope of the "corresponding" consumption-indifference curve at the "corresponding" point. In terms of Figure I the slope of I_t at Q is the same as the slope of I_c at S. This can be proved as follows. When the corner of the production block moves from Q to Q ', the vertical component of the movement is made up of the vertical component in the movement of the point of tangency along the I_c-curve from S to T (which we will call a') plus the vertical component in the movement of the point of tangency along the production block from S' to T (which we will call a). In other words more B-exportables are imported into A (i) because more B-exportables are consumed in A (equal to a') and (ii) because less B-exportables are produced in A (equal to a). Similarly the horizontal component in the movement from Q to Q' is equal to the horizontal component in the movement along the I_c-curve (b') plus the horizontal component in the movement along the production block (b).

The slope of the I_t-curve between Q and Q' equals $\dfrac{a + a'}{b + b'}$. If we now let Q' approach Q, $\dfrac{a}{b}$ approaches the slope of the tangent to the production block and $\dfrac{a'}{b'}$ approaches the slope of the tangent to the I_c-curve; and at the point S these two slopes are equal to each other.

But where $\dfrac{a}{b} = \dfrac{a'}{b'}$ it follows that $\dfrac{a}{b} = \dfrac{a'}{b'} = \dfrac{a + a'}{b + b'}$.* In other words at the point Q the slope of the I_t-curve is equal to the slope of the I_c-curve and to the slope of the production block at the point S.

(ii) It follows that if I_c is always negatively sloped, I_t will always be negatively sloped, since each point on I_t has a slope which is equal to the slope of some corresponding point on I_c.

(iii) It also follows that, in the case of increasing costs as shown in Figure I, if I_c is always convex, I_t will always be convex. From Figure I we can see that if the slope of I_c increases as one moves from S to T, the slope of I_t will increase as one moves from Q to Q'.

(iv) In the quadrant X'OY there is a closely packed family of I_c-curves. Each of these curves may be asymptotic to the axes OX' and OY, or in other words whatever their incomes and the market price relationships may be, consumers in A may always insist on purchasing something of both commodities. But if the production block in A has any finite height as well as a finite breadth, there will always be one position of the production block at which it will be tangential to an I_c-curve and its corner will coincide with the origin O. In other words there will always be an I_t-curve which passes through O like the curve marked I_t in Figure I. All lower I_t-curves will cut the OX axis (even though no I_c-curve cuts the OX' axis), and all higher I_t-curves will cut the OY axis.

(v) If in the map of A's consumption-indifference curves neither commodity is at any point an inferior good, then in the map of A's trade-indifference curves

---

* $\dfrac{a + a'}{b + b'} = \dfrac{a\left(1 + \dfrac{a'}{a}\right)}{b\left(1 + \dfrac{b'}{b}\right)}$. But if $\dfrac{a}{b} = \dfrac{a'}{b'}$, it follows that $\dfrac{a'}{a} = \dfrac{b'}{b}$, so that $\dfrac{a + a'}{b + b'} = \dfrac{a}{b}$

neither commodity will be at any point an inferior good. The geometric meaning of this statement can be seen from Figure II; its economic significance will become clearer in the arguments which follow.

We will define the absence of inferior goods in A's consumption as the condition in which, if the incomes of A's consumers rise and price relationships remain the same, A's consumers will purchase more of both commodities. In Figure II suppose that the incomes of A's consumers measured in terms of A-exportables rise from OC to OD, the price of B-exportables in terms of A-importables remaining unchanged (i.e. the slope of the price line CP being the same as that of the price line DT). A's consumers in the first position move up the price line CP to P, the point at which it is tangential to the curve I_c^1. In the second position they move up the price line DT to T, where it is tangential to I_c^4. The absence of inferior goods means that T will lie North of P (because more B-exportables will be consumed) and West of P (because more A-exportables will be consumed).

Draw a vertical line EF passing through the point P and cutting the line DT at P'. It is clear that since T is to the West of EF and since I_c-curves are negatively sloped and convex, the I_c-curve which passes through P' (I_c^2) will at P' have a steeper slope than the line DP'. We can say then that, if there are no inferior goods, as we move up any vertical line EF we shall cut steeper and steeper I_c-curves. We wish to prove that the I_t-curves have a similar property.

Place the production block PQ in position tangentially to I_c^1 at P. Q is the corresponding point on the corresponding I_t-curve, $I_{t'}^1$, which at this point will have a slope equal to that of the price line CP. Slide the production block northwards until P coincides with P', the point of intersection of EF and DT; and Q will then have moved an equal distance northwards to Q'. Since the slope of the production block at P equalled the slope of CP, the slope of the production block at P′ will equal the slope of the same price line DP′. Q′ will not therefore be the point in the trade-indifference map which corresponds to the point P′ in the consumption-indifference map, since the production block is not tangential to I_c^2 at P′. The production block will be tangential to I_c^3 at S, and at S the slope of the production block will be steeper than at P′. In other words the slope at S is steeper than at P, so that the slope of I_t^3 at Q′ is steeper than that of I_t^1 at Q. In other words if we move directly northwards (e.g. from Q to Q′) through the trade-indifference map the higher and higher trade-indifference curves which we shall cut will have steeper and steeper slopes.

Similarly it could be shown that in the absence of inferior goods in A's consumption (i) the successive consumption-indifference curves which one would cut as one ploughed due West through the consumption-indifference map would be less and less steeply sloped, and (ii) the successive trade-indifference curves which one would cut as one ploughed due West through the trade-indifference map would also be less and less steeply sloped.

These geometrical properties we shall call the absence of inferior goods.

(vi) Suppose the production block were the rectangle RPUO (Figure I). This would mean that in A there was the fixed output RP of B-exportables and PU of A-exportables. The curve I_t would then be exactly parallel to the curve I_c, each point Q on every I_t-curve lying exactly PR to the South and PU to the East of the corresponding point S on the corresponding I_c-curve.

A special case would be where in A only A-exportables and no B-exportables could be produced. The production block would take the form of the line PU. Then I_t would be traced out parallel to I_c and exactly PU to the East of it at each point. If I_c were asymptotic to OX′, I_t would

16

be asymptotic to XX'. This would give us the familiar geometric construction where for trade purposes we could draw the A-consumption-indifference map in the quadrant YOX using XO for the axis OX' and a vertical axis a distance PU to the East of OY in place of OY.

(vii) We can now show the general effect upon the slope of the I_t-curves of allowing for the fact that producers in A can shift from the production of A-exportables to that of B-exportables and vice versa. Consider the point S in Figure I on the curve I_c and the corresponding point Q on I_t. Suppose that the production block took the form of a rectangle with S and Q as its opposite corners. Then when the production block moved North through a distance equal to the northerly component in the movement from Q to Q', S' (which is the point on the production block in its new position corresponding to S) would have to be kept tangential to I_c. In other words Q' would be further to the West than is the case in Figure I. The slope of I_t at Q is equal to the slope of I_c at S, and is therefore unchanged whether the production block be of the shape actually shown in Figure I or a rectangle SQ. But if it were a rectangle SQ, then Q' would move further to the West. In other words lessening of the concavity of the production block will remove the parallelism between the I_t-curve and the I_c-curve and will make the I_t-curve less convex than the corresponding I_c-curve. Moreover, the less concave the production block, the less convex will the I_t-curve be as compared with the corresponding I_c-curve.

(viii) Consider the point at which the production block in Figure I has moved up the curve I_c to the point E at which the slope of I_c is equal to the slope of the production block at its steepest point P'. Then the corresponding point F on I_t will lie directly to the right of E by a distance equal to P'O. From this point onwards the trade-indifference move will be exactly parallel to

the consumption-indifference curve, but at a distance EF
(= P'O) to the right. Similarly, when the production-
block has moved down I_c to the point H at which the
slope of I_c is equal to the slope of the production block
at its corner P'', the remainder of I_t (i.e. to the left of G)
is exactly parallel to the remainder of I_c (i.e. to the left
of H) but a distance HG (= P''O) below I_c. Thus the
trade-indifference curve I_t is made up of three parts.
First, the part to the left of G which exactly reproduces
the part of I_c lying to the left of H. Second, the part
above F which exactly reproduces the part of I_c lying
above E. Third, the intermediate part, FG, which "dis-
torts" the intermediate part of I_c (i.e. EH) in the way
described above. At F and G there are discontinuities,
not in the slope of I_t, but in the rate of change of the
slope of I_t. At the point F the slope of I_t is unequivocally
equal to the slope of I_c at E. But just before F the slope
of I_t is changing at a rate affected by the rates of change
in the slopes of I_c and of the production block; and just
after F the rate of change of the slope of I_t is equal to
the rate of change of the slope of I_c.

CHAPTER III

The Free Trade Equilibrium with a Zero Balance of Trade

WE can next show how this trade-indifference map can be used for the purpose of analysing problems of international trade. Consider on Figure III the positions indicated by the successive price lines α^0 and α^1. With α^1, a relatively large amount of B-exportables (measured on the Y-axis) can be obtained for a given amount of A-exportables (measured on the X-axis); but with α^0, only a relatively small amount of B-exportables can be obtained for the same amount of A-exportables. Thus as the price line α becomes steeper and steeper the price of A-exportables rises relatively to that of B-exportables and the terms of trade move in favour of A-exportables.

We are assuming (see point (iv) on page 14 above) that there is a trade-indifference curve which passes through O. At O this curve has the slope α^0, which (see point (i) on page 13 above) will also measure the price relationship in A between A-exportables and B-exportables in the absence of any international trade. Now let α^0 move round to α^1. The new price line will be tangential to a higher A-trade indifference curve (I_t^1 in Figure III). The locus of the points of tangency between successive price lines and A-trade-indifference curves traces out A's offer curve (O_a).

This offer curve has the familiar properties of the offer curve which is normally used in the analysis of international trade. Consider the point Q on O_a. Place A's production block GQ in position with its corner at Q. Then by the nature of the construction of the trade-indifference curve I_t^1, the production block will be tangential to an A-consumption-indifference curve (I_c^1)

at a point (G in Figure III) at which the production block and the consumption-indifference curve both have a slope equal to the slope of the trade-indifference curve at Q (i.e. α_2^1 has the same slope as α^1). Through G draw the vertical line GC cutting the base of the production block at F, and through F draw a price line α_1^1, parallel to α^1 and α_2^1, cutting OX' at D.

Now the total output in A of A-exportables is FQ or DO. The output of B-exportables is only GF, which is equal in value in terms of A-exportables to ED, since α_2^1 and α_1^1 both measure the rate at which GF can be converted into A-exportables. The income which A-consumers have to spend, measured in terms of A-exportables, is therefore equal to EO (i.e. DO + DE). This they can spend on the price line α_2^1, until they reach their highest consumption-indifference curve I_c^1 at G.

They will thus consume GC of B-exportables; but only GF is made in A so that FC or HO measures A's imports. They will consume FH of A-exportables; but FQ is produced in A so that HQ measures A's exports. But the point Q is on the intersection of A's offer curve (O_a) and the price line α^1 the slope of which itself is equal to the terms of trade (i.e. A's imports $\div$ by A's exports or $\frac{OH}{HQ}$). We can conclude that if we take any point Q on A's offer curve as we have derived it, then HQ will represent the amount of imports which A's producers will offer and HO the amount of imports which A's consumers will demand at a price corresponding to $\frac{OH}{HQ}$. The curve O_a has the normal properties of an international-trade offer curve.

We have seen that α^0 represents the price relationship that would rule in the absence of international trade. Suppose now that the price relationship fell to α^{-1}, i.e. to a position still more disadvantageous to A-exportables.

It would pay traders in A now to *export* "B-exportables" and to *import* "A-exportables," as can be seen from the point of tangency of α^{-1} with I_t^1 at L. Thus A's offer curve passes from the quadrant XOY where it pays A to export A-exportables and to import B-exportables, through O where there is no incentive to trade, into the quadrant X'OY' where it pays A to *export* "B-export-ables" and to *import* "A-exportables." The point L lies on the same trade-indifference curve as the point Q. In other words, if in a situation of no-trade (the price relationship being α^0) international trade is opened up, A will gain provided that the new price relationship differs from the old. A gains as much by a movement of the price of A-exportables downwards from α^0 to α^{-1} as she does from a movement upwards from α^0 to α^1.

We have seen that the quadrant X'OY can be used to measure consumption in A and the quadrants XOY and X'OY' to measure A's foreign trade, according as to which commodity is exported and which imported. We can now make use of the quadrant XOY' to measure consumption in B, so that the quadrants X'OY' and XOY can measure B's foreign trade also. We shall then have an apparatus for expressing the mutual trading relations between A and B.

Consider the quadrant XOY' in Figure IV. Along OY' measure the amount of B-exportables consumed in B, and along OX the amount of A-exportables consumed in B. We have then a family of B-consumption-indifference curves of which I_{cb} is one. Now place the B-production block QK tangentially against I_{cb} with its A-exportable base horizontal and its B-exportable base vertical. Slide it along I_{cb}. Its corner Q will trace out the corresponding B-trade-indifference curve I_{tb}, of which there will be a family in the quadrants YOX and X'OY'. Draw successive price lines α through O, and let O_b or B's offer curve trace out the locus of the points at which the various price lines are tangential to B-trade-indifference curves.

If there is free trade and no surplus or deficit in the balance of trade, then the position of trade equilibrium will be determined at the point Q at which A's and B's offer curves intersect. The point of consumption in A will be at E where the slope of the price line α_2, which is equal to the slope of A's consumption-indifference curve and of A's production block, is equal to the terms of international trade α. Consumers in A will consume OC (or DG) of A-exportables leaving GQ for export. They will consume OF and produce GF of B-exportables, requiring OG from imports: GQ will thus be exported and OG imported. In B consumers will consume OH (or MJ) of B-exportables, leaving MQ (or OG) for export: and they will consume OL of A-exportables, requiring OM (or GQ) from imports. At the consumption point K the slope of B's production block and consumption-indifference curve α_1 is also the same as that of the international terms of trade (α).

Figure IV thus shows the final free-trade equilibrium between A and B in the absence of any surplus or deficit in the balance of trade. It may, however, be useful at this point to explain the fundamental properties of the four quadrants and of the points O and Q which will normally* be used throughout the rest of this book, whether we are dealing with positions of free trade or protection or of the absence or the presence of balance-of-trade deficits.

These properties are illustrated in Figure V. Take A's production block QLM and B's production block QPN: place them corner to corner with the A-exportable base of both production blocks in a horizontal position and the B-exportable base of both production blocks in a vertical position, as in the Figure. Then the blocks' axes

* That is to say, in all Figures except Figures XIX and XX.

MP and LN represent the *production* axes with their origin at Q. Take any two points S and T on the edges of the A- and the B-production blocks respectively. Complete the rectangle SVTU. Then this is the production box. SV of B-exportables is now being *produced* (HQ in A and KQ in B); and SU of A-exportables is being *produced* (GQ in A and QJ in B). If now we shift our attention to the axes YY' amd XX' with their origin at O, then the points S and T mean that SV of B-exportables is being *consumed* (OD in A and OF in B); and SU of A-exportables is being *consumed* (CO in A and OE in B). Thus RQ is A's exports and OR is B's exports.

$\dfrac{RQ}{OR}$ will thus always measure the *gross* barter terms of trade between A and B. In Figure IV it measures also the net barter terms of trade, the market price relationship between the two commodities within A, and the market price relationship between the two commodities in B. But it need not measure any of these three other things. It will not measure the net barter terms of trade if there is a surplus or deficit in the balance of trade; for in the case in which some exports are not currently paid for by imports, the ratio of total exports to total imports will not be equal to the ratio at which exports will exchange for imports at the current prices. Nor will the terms of international trade measure the price relationships within each country if there are import or export duties or subsidies.

In Figure V we show Q as lying North-East of O. From the argument explaining Figures III and IV it is clear that in the free trade conditions with no deficit or surplus in the balance of trade Q must lie North-East or South-West of O, according as to which commodity is imported and which exported from A. But if the balance of trade is not zero there is no reason why Q might not lie North-West or South-East of O. Suppose that reparations or Marshall Aid or ordinary capital lending is transferred from B to A on a very large scale and that, in the absence of international trade or transfers, the price relationship between A-exportables and B-exportables would be very similar in both countries. Then the result might be that both commodities flowed from B to A to finance the transfer of gifts or lending from B to A. Q would lie to the North-West of O; consumption of both commodities would be greater than production in A and less than production in B.

Figures VI, VII, and VIII illustrate the most familiar international conditions for the maximization of welfare. In Figure VI at S the slope of the production block in A (α), is less steep than the slope of the production block in B (β). Supposing now that B gives up a small amount of production of A-exportables, moving along the B-production block to T'; and suppose that A produces an equivalent amount more of A-exportables, moving along the A-production block to S'. (The horizontal distance between S and S' is assumed to be the same as the horizontal distance between T and T', so that SU = VT = S'U' = V'T'.) Then the vertical distance between T and T' will be greater than the vertical distance between S and S', because β (which approximates to the slope of the B-production block between T and T') is steeper than α (which approximates to the slope of the A-production block between S and S'). In consequence U'T' will be greater than UT. In other words if the slopes of the production blocks in the two countries differ it will be possible for the two countries by a reshuffling of their productive resources among the two industries to produce more of the one commodity without producing less of the other.

Figure VII illustrates the case where the slope (α) of the A-consumption-indifference curve (I_{ca}) at the A-consumption point S is less steep than the slope (β) of the B-consumption-indifference curve at the B-consumption point T. Keep the production of both commodities in both countries constant, so that the production box SUTV remains constant with its origin Q. Now let the corner T of this production box slide up the curve I_{cb} to T', so that Q, V, U, and S will all move to an equal extent in the same north-easterly direction. It is clear that the new A-consumption point S' will lie on a higher A-consumption-indifference curve, because the slope of α at S (which is equal to the slope of I_{ca} at S) is less than the slope of β at T (which approximates to the slope of I_{cb} between T and T'). In other words when the slope of the consumption-indifference curves are different in two countries, the consumers can be made better off in the one country without the consumers in the other being made worse off by means of a different exchange of a constant output of commodities.

In Figure VIII there are neither of the possibilities of improvement which existed in Figures VI and VII. At A's production point S the slope (α_1) of A's production block is the same as the slope (β_1) of B's production block at B's production point T. And at A's consumption point S the slope (α_2) of A's consumption-indifference curve (I_{ca}^1) is the same as the slope (β_2) of B's consumption-indifference curve (I_{cb}^1) at B's consumption point T. But if trade remained the same (the origin Q remaining unchanged in relation to the origin O), the consumers in both countries could be made better off if in each country rather more A-exportables and less B-exportables were produced and consumed. It is clear that as α_2 is steeper than α_1 a movement of A's production-consumption point from S to S' will bring A's consumers into the higher consumption-indifference curve I_{ca}^2. And similarly in B with a movement of production and consumption from T to T'.

It follows that welfare will be maximized in the very

limited sense of its being impossible to increase the welfare of the citizens in one country without reducing the welfare of the citizens in the other, if the slope of A's production block equals the slope of A's consumption-indifference curve equals the slope of B's production block equals the slope of B's consumption-indifference curve. The position of free trade, without any balance-of-trade deficit or surplus, illustrated in Figure IV, may be seen to provide one example of the fulfilment of these conditions.

These few observations are not, of course, intended to be a complete account of the problems of economic welfare in international trade. They need to be supplemented in at least two ways.

First, as will be seen in Chapter V in the discussion of decreasing costs, the fulfilment of the conditions just discussed in connection with Figures VI to VIII may mean only that we are at some point of local optimum. A small change in either direction would make the situation worse. But a large structural change might bring the economy to a still higher local peak.

Second, the analysis here presented takes no account of the distribution of the world income between citizens of A and citizens of B. It shows merely the conditions in which one set of citizens *could* be made better off without the other being made worse off. But a change of policy, while it may move the economy from a position in which it was possible to a position in which it is no longer possible to make the one set of citizens better off without making the other worse off, may in fact so redistribute income as to make one set better off and the other worse off than they were in the first position. And if the actual deterioration of the position of the latter is in some sense greater than the actual improvement of the position of the former the change may be in fact undesirable. This point will be considered further in discussing Figure LI.

CHAPTER IV

The Case of Constant Costs

BEFORE we proceed with our general argument, it may be worth while pausing to consider how the general free trade zero-trade-balance equilibrium shown in Figure IV would be modified if there were constant costs instead of increasing costs. The derivation of the trade-indifference curves and so of the offer curve of any country under conditions of constant costs is shown in Figure IX.

When there are constant costs in country A the production block, instead of being of the shape of OP'PP''O in Figure I becomes a triangle such as COD in Figure IX. OC measures the total amount of B-exportables which A could produce if she produced no A-exportables, and OD measures the total amount of A-exportables which A could produce if she produced no B-exportables. Since there are constant costs, i.e. a constant rate of transformation of A-exportables into B-exportables, the production possibilities in A lie along the straight line CED, the slope of which measures the constant cost of the one product in terms of the other. In the closed economy the production and consumption equilibrium inside A will be determined at the point E at which the production line CD is tangential to the consumption-indifference curve I_c.

We can now derive the trade-indifference curves of A. Let the production triangle COD slide up to the North-East, keeping CD tangential to I_c at the point E. The right-angled corner of the production triangle will trace out the straight dotted line OF until the point D of the triangle has reached the point E on I_c and the triangle COD is in the position shown by the thin lines in Figure IX. The straight dotted line OF therefore represents the first part of the trade-indifference curve I_t which corresponds to the consumption-indifference curve I_c. After this point all resources in A are devoted to the production of A-exportables and the single straight line EF ($=$ DO) now represents the production block. The point E now slides up the consumption-indifference curve and the point F now traces out a section of the trade-indifference curve (F to I_t) which is exactly parallel to the corresponding section of the consumption-indifference curve (E to I_c) but a distance EF or DO to the East of it. Similarly, if the production triangle COD is slid downwards, the right-angled corner of the production triangle at first traces out the straight dotted line OG until the point is reached at G at which the corner of the triangle is exactly below E, and from that point onwards the I_t-curve is exactly parallel to the I_c-curve but a constant distance (EG or CO) below it.*

By a similar process a family of A-trade-indifference curves can be described. Take any other consumption-indifference curve I_c'; choose the point E' on this curve at which the slope of I_c' is the same as the slope of DC; take the point F' immediately East of E' by a distance DO and the point G' immediately South of E' by a distance CO; join G' and F' to form the straight-line part of the corresponding trade-indifference curve I_t' To the North-East of F', I_t' will be exactly parallel to I_c' but a distance DO ($=$ E'F') to the East, and to the South-West of G', I_t' will be exactly parallel to I_c' but a distance CO ($=$ E'G') below it.

We can now derive the A-offer curve (O_a) from the A-trade-indifference curves. The price line α, which has the same slope as DC and which passes through O, will

---

* In terms of Figure I it is as if the points E and H on I_c were brought nearer and nearer together until they coincided. The points F and G on I_t are thus brought nearer together but do not coincide. They are joined together by a straight line having a slope equal to the slope of I_c at the point at which E and H coincide.

have the same slope as OF, the straight-line part of the trade-indifference curve I_t. OF will, therefore, also describe the first part of A's offer curve, which is the locus of all points at which a price line through O is tangential to a trade-indifference curve. A steeper price line through O, such as α' in Figure IX, will be tangential to the higher trade-indifference curve I_t' at a point such as H North-East of F'.*

The point H will, therefore, be on A's offer curve. This offer curve will thus be of the shape of the continuous line OFO_a, i.e. a straight section OF with a discontinuity at F, from which point it will trace out the curved type of offer curve which is represented in the normal diagrams (cf. Figures III and IV).†

The distinguishing feature of constant costs is, therefore, the fact that over the first part of its distance from the origin O the offer curve will be a straight line and will then break discontinuously into a more normally curved offer curve. The actual importance of this fact depends very much upon the length of the straight-line part of the offer curve; and in Figures X and XI we attempt to illustrate the two most important factors determining the length of the straight-line section of the offer curve.

Figure X illustrates the rather obvious point that the larger is country A the greater will be the length of the straight-line section of the offer curve. In Figure X two situations are depicted, the only difference between them being that the production and consumption conditions

---

* There is no discontinuity in the slope of I_t' at F', only in the rate of change of the slope. The point of tangency of α' with I_t' cannot therefore be at F' (which has the same slope as α) but must be North-East of F'.

† The conditions (i) to (viii) (pp. 13–18) laid down about the nature of the trade-indifference curves were based upon the assumption of increasing costs. With constant costs, conditions (iii) and (v) would need some modification. Over the straight-line sections of the trade-indifference curves (GF and G'F' of Figure IX), I_t is not convex and a vertical line which cuts both GF and G'F' will not cut trade-indifference curves with higher and higher slopes.

in A in the one case are both 50 per cent larger than in the other case. Thus the production triangles have the same shape but C'C is 50 per cent of CO and D'D is 50 per cent of DO. E is the point of equilibrium with the smaller production triangle DCO. On the production line D'C' in the larger position we have chosen a consumption point E' which lies on the straight line passing through O and E. This means that we have assumed that the proportion of total expenditure devoted to each commodity is the same in each situation*, so that consumption also is merely larger all round but otherwise unchanged. By similar triangles, one can see that $\frac{C'O}{CO} \left(= \frac{D'O}{DO}\right) = \frac{E'O}{EO} = \frac{F'O}{FO}$. In other words, if A is a 50 per cent bigger economy FO will be 50 per cent longer.

Figure XI illustrates the slightly less obvious point that given the size of total productive resources in A the straight-line section of A's offer curve will be the longer, the smaller is the proportion of total expenditure in A which is devoted to A-exportables. The point E in Figure XI shows a position in which the demand in A for A-exportables is large and that for B-exportables small as compared with the point E'; in all other respects the two positions are identical. It is clear from the diagram that OF will be shorter than OF'. The straight-line section of A's offer curve is increased by a shift of demand in A away from A-exportables on to B-exportables.

In Figure XII we put together the offer curves of two countries in both of which there are constant costs. Both offer curves accordingly have straight-line sections. We show two offer curves for A; in the one offer curve the straight-line section is shorter than in the other. Now it

* By similar triangles $\frac{GO}{GD} = \frac{G'O}{D'O} =$ the ratio of expenditure on A-exportables to expenditure on B-exportables.

is clear that the trade-equilibrium point may lie (as at Q) at a point at which the terms of trade (α) lie between the slopes of the straight-line sections of the two offer curves. But if the straight-line section of A's offer curve is sufficiently long and of B's sufficiently short, the trade-equilibrium point will lie (as at Q') at a point on the straight-line section of A's offer curve so that the terms of trade (α') coincide with the slope of the straight-line section of A's offer curve. This will be the case if A's economy is large relatively to B's and if A-exportables are in much smaller demand than B-exportables in both countries. In such a case if the large country A devoted all its resources to the production of the commodity (A-exportables) for which the total demand was very small, the market would be swamped with A-exportables and starved of B-exportables. The large country must produce something of the important commodity.

From Figures XII and IX it can be seen that if the trade equilibrium is at Q' (Figure XII) then the consumption point in A will be at E (Figure IX), i.e. exactly at the point at which it would have been had there been no international trade. All that has happened in A is that the production triangle COD (Figure IX) has slid a little way North-East with the line CD remaining tangential to I_c at E; A is producing a little more A-exportables and less B-exportables, but she is exporting the whole of her excess output of A-exportables and is replacing all her deficiency of B-exportables by imports from B. She gains nothing from the trade. The whole gain goes to the small country or to the country which produces the commodity which is in heavy demand.*

* This is, of course, merely a geometrical representation of the criticism which Professor F. D. Graham has forcibly made of the classical theory of the influence of reciprocal demand in international trade.

CHAPTER V

The Case of Decreasing Costs

IN the previous chapter we considered how the argument might be affected if in each of our two countries there were constant costs in the sense that the additional amount of A-exportables which could be produced if one unit less of B-exportables was produced remained constant,* regardless of the total amount of each commodity which is in fact being produced. The marginal rate of substitution in production between A-exportables and B-exportables is constant.

In this chapter we will say something of the case of decreasing costs. Let us suppose that either in the industry producing A-exportables or in the industry producing B-importables there are increasing returns to scale so that the very fact that the total scale of operations is increased causes a reduction in real cost of production. There will now be two conflicting tendencies at work. As, for example, the output of A-exportables is increased and that of B-exportables decreased, (i) there will be an increased demand for those factors of production which are particularly important for the production of A-exportables and a fall in the demand for those factors which are particularly important for the production of B-exportables; and the price of the former will rise and of the latter will fall, so that the cost of A-exportables will tend to rise relatively to that of B-exportables, but (ii) as the total scale of production of A-exportables increases the real cost of production in that industry will tend to fall in so far as there are economies of large-scale production, while real costs may rise in the production of B-exportables as their output is contracted. If tendency

* Assuming, of course, that something of each commodity is being produced.

(ii) outweighs tendency (i) then we have a case of decreasing costs. The larger is the output of A-exportables and the smaller is the output of B-exportables, the lower is the amount of B-exportables which must be given up in production in order to release the resources necessary to produce one more unit of A-exportables.

It is a familiar proposition that such increasing returns are likely to be associated with conditions of monopoly. But in this chapter we intend to maintain the assumption that there is perfect competition or, perhaps more accurately, that the economic system behaves as if there were perfect competition. We wish to assume, that is to say, that on the production side prices are equal to marginal costs and that commodities are sold in free markets. This we can justify by assuming *either* that the economies of scale are external to the individual firms and that there is a system of taxes and subsidies which equates price to marginal social cost in each competitive industry, *or* that the economies of scale are internal to large monopolistic firms and that the State controls each industry in such a way that it produces up to the point at which the price is equal to the marginal social cost of production.

We can now draw our production blocks of the shape shown as CDQ in Figure XIII, where CQ represents the amount of A-exportables which would be produced if all resources were used to produce A-exportables and DQ represents the amount of B-exportables which could be produced if all resources were used for their production. The line CD is convex instead of concave to show that the marginal cost of A-exportables in terms of B-exportables falls as more A-exportables are produced. We are interested only in the parts of the line CD at which it is less convex than the relevant points on the relevant consumption-indifference curves. At any position of equilibrium in domestic consumption and

production the line CD must be tangential to a consumption-indifference curve as at H in Figure XIII; and in
order that this position should be one of stable equilibrium the convexity of I_c at H must be greater than
the convexity of CD. If (i) the consumption-indifference
curves are asymptotic to the X and Y axes, i.e. if consumers always want to have at least some small amount
of each commodity, and (ii) if the total amount of either
commodity which could be produced is a finite quantity
even though all resources are devoted to it, there will
always be such positions of stable equilibrium as can be
seen from Figure XIII. Even if there were sections of
the production block such as EF in Figure XIII where
the convexity of the production block was greater than
that of the consumption-indifference curves, yet the facts
that I_c is asymptotic to the two axes while the production
block is not, means that there must be points of tangency
such as H and G where the production block is tangential
to consumption-indifference curves and where the convexity of the former is less than that of the latter.

We can show in Figure XIV how in this case the
trade-indifference curves are derived from the consumption-indifference curves when all points on the
production block are less convex than all points with
similar slopes on all consumption-indifference curves.
Consider the consumption-indifference curve I_c and the
production block CQD. The problem is to derive the
trade-indifference curve I_t. Take the point E on I_c at
which the slope of I_c is equal to the slope of the production block at the point C. If the point C of the
production block now slides up I_c, the corner Q of the
production block will trace out the line LMI_t. This is
the portion of the trade-indifference curve which corresponds to I_c when country A produces only CQ of
A-exportables.

Similarly, take the point F where the slope of I_c equals

34

the slope of the production block at the point D. Slide D down I_c, and the corner Q of the production block will trace out a line KJ and onwards which is exactly parallel to FE and onwards. This is the portion of the trade-indifference curve which corresponds to I_c when country A produces only DQ of B-exportables. It is interesting to observe that both JK and LM reproduce exactly the same section EF of I_c. The part of the trade-indifference curve up to K reproduces the consumption-indifference curve up to F; the part of the trade-indifference curve beyond M reproduces the consumption-indifference curve beyond F; the remaining section of the trade-indifference curve—namely, between K and M—is filled partly by a repetition of the section JK between L and M. This leaves a section KL still unfilled.

This is the section of the trade indifference curve which corresponds to the portion of I_c between E and F when country A is producing something of both commodities. It has the following characteristics. Consider the point of tangency H between I_c and CD. This gives the point Q on the trade-indifference curve between K and L. And by proposition (i) on page 13 the slope of KL at the point Q will be the same as the slope of I_c at the point H. If now Q moves up in a north-easterly direction to Q' it is clear that the point of tangency between I_c and C'D' moves in a south-westerly direction to G, and the slope of I_t at Q' will be equal to the slope of I_c at G. It follows that the slope of I_t at Q' will be less steep than the slope of I_t at Q. In other words, in the decreasing cost case each trade-indifference curve will be made up of two normally convex sections corresponding to the situations in which the country is concentrating solely on the production of one or the other commodity, but these convex sections will be joined together by a concave section corresponding to the situation in which the country is producing something

35

of both commodities. At K and L, the points of junction of these sections, there will be no discontinuity in the slope of I_t, but there will be a discontinuity in the rate of change of the slope of I_t.

It can be seen that if there is a part of the production block, such as between H and G in Figure XV, which is more convex than the relevant points on the consumption-indifference curve, then as the block CQD slides up and down I_c, there will be at least one position of double tangency. This is shown in Figure XV where the line CD is tangential to I_c at the points H and G simultaneously. Inspection of Figure XV shows that at the point Q which corresponds on I_t both to H and to G on I_c there will be a sharp discontinuity in the slope of I_t. F is the point on I_c at which the slope of I_c is equal to the slope of CD at its steepest point D. When D is to the left of F on I_c, I_t will be exactly parallel to I_c and Q will lie on I_t to the left of K. As the production block slides further up, its points of tangency with I_c will lie on I_c between F and G, and so the slope of any point on I_t between K and Q will be equal to that of some corresponding point on I_c between F and G. But after the point of double tangency, shown in Figure XV, the slope of any point on I_t between Q and L will be equal to that of some corresponding point on I_c between H and E. Thus there will be a sharp break in the slope of I_t at Q, at which point the slope of I_t must be equal to the slope of I_c at both G and H.

In Figure XVI we show how to derive the offer curve from trade-indifference curves of this shape. Draw a price line α through O which has a slope equal to the slope of the production block at its corner C (Figure XIV). All the trade-indifference curves will have a slope equal to α at the points of inflexion L (Figure XIV) at which their slopes cease to decrease and start to increase. In Figure XVI, therefore, the price line α will be tangential to some trade-indifference curve at such a point, i.e. at E. This will be a point on A's offer curve O_a. Now it is clear that if the price line α had a lower slope there would be no point of tangency between it and a trade-indifference curve in the neighbourhood of E, since (Figure XIV) L is the point of lowest slope of the trade-indifference curve until we move right down to the point J. But there will be points of tangency of the price line α and of price lines less steeply sloped than α in the region of the point F in Figure XVI.

But now let the price line become a little steeper at α'. There will now be two points of tangency in the region of E, one at D on the concave part of a trade-indifference curve and one at C on the convex part of a trade-indifference curve. There will be another point of tangency to α' at G, in the region of F.

Similarly, one can draw a line β which has the same slope as the production block if country A produced only B-exportables. It would be tangential to a trade-indifference curve at a point of inflexion at H. Thus by swinging the price lines α and β round the origin O we can trace out an A-offer curve of the shape of O_a in Figure XVI. The slope of this offer curve at the origin O will, of course, be equal to the slope of the "no-trade" trade-indifference curve which passes through that point. It will have two sharp discontinuities at H and E.

In Figures XVII and XVIII we put together such an offer curve for country A (O_a) with a similar offer curve for country B (O_b). It will be seen that there are likely to be at least three points of intersection, Q_1, Q_2, and Q_3. In Figure XVII Q_1 is the point of equilibrium when A produces only A-exportables and B only B-exportables; Q_2 the point when A produces only B-exportables and B only A-exportables; and Q_3 the point when both produce both. Thus in Figure XVII Q_1 and Q_2 are points of complete specialization in both countries. But suppose that one country (e.g. country B) were very much smaller than the other country (country A); then in order that the world market might not be starved of either commodity it might well be necessary for A to produce something of both commodities in all positions of equilibrium. This position is illustrated in Figure XVIII, where Q_1, Q_2, and Q_3 are all positions of equilibrium in which A produces both commodities; but at Q_1 B specializes wholly on the production of B-exportables, at Q_2 B specializes wholly on the production of A-exportables, and at Q_3 B also produces something of each commodity.

Let us consider first the positions of total specialization shown in Figure XVII.* On this Figure Q_1 and Q_2 are points at which each country is producing only one product. Since each country is producing a fixed amount of only one product the ordinary rules for stability discussed below on pp. 91–92 will hold good for points Q_1 and Q_2 of Figure XVII. They are, therefore, not only positions of equilibrium but also, as they are drawn, positions of stable equilibrium.†

But the problem is different for the point Q_3. Q_3 is a pessimum, and not an optimum, point, since on the contract curve K_3 the A-trade-indifference curve is concave and the B-trade-indifference curve is convex. This is simply the geometrical representation of the fact that if A produced more of one commodity (it does not matter which) and B more of the other, then because of increasing returns to scale more of both commodities would be produced and both countries could be better off. It can be seen from Figure XVII that a small move-

* It can be seen from the shape of the trade-indifference curves which lie behind the offer curves that there are three contract curves K_1, K_2, and K_3, corresponding to the three positions of total specialization or of non-specialization. For the definition of the contract curve, see page 65 below.

† In the region of the point Q_1 or Q_2 the two offer curves *might* intersect in the way shown in Figure XXVII. If they did so, then two of the positions of equilibrium would be stable and the other unstable.

ment North-East or South-West from Q_3 will get both A and B on to a higher trade-indifference curve, and on certain assumptions Q_3 is, in fact, a point of unstable equilibrium. Thus suppose that the world economy does start in equilibrium at the point Q_3 in Figure XVII. Suppose then that there is some small accidental increase in the production of A-exportables and decrease in the production of B-exportables in A combined with some small accidental shift of resources in the opposite direction in A. There may not be any marked change in the world market demand price of either product since the increased supply of A-exportables in A will be accompanied by a decreased supply of A-exportables in B; and vice versa with B-exportables. But because of increasing returns to scale the marginal cost of A-exportables in A will have fallen and the marginal cost of B-exportables in A will have risen; and if, therefore, the prices of the two products have not much altered there will be an incentive in A to increase still further the output of A-exportables and to decrease still further the output of B-exportables. At the same time producers in B, because of increasing returns to scale, will have an incentive to increase still further the output of B-exportables and to decrease still further the output of A-exportables. Starting from the equilibrium position Q_3 a small accidental jolt in either direction will cause the world economy to move off either to Q_1 or to Q_2.*

Arguments, such as the above, about conditions of stability and instability usually rest explicitly or implicitly upon some assumptions about the dynamic processes which are set in motion when an equilibrium is disturbed; and the nature of these dynamic processes depends in turn *inter alia* upon the time-lags between various

---

* I am indebted to Mr. R. C. O. Matthews' article entitled "Reciprocal Demand and the Terms of Trade" in the *Review of Economic Studies*, Vol. XVII (2) for the above argument.

changes and their repercussions. It is possible to imagine a condition of time-lags which would have the result of making the position Q_3 less unstable than is suggested above. Suppose for example that the economies of large-scale production developed only after a considerable time. When in country A the output of A-exportables is increased and the output of B-exportables is decreased, the immediate short-run effect is that the marginal cost of the former rises and of the latter falls, because of the changed factor proportions required in the two productions. It is only after a considerable period of larger-scale production of A-exportables and of smaller-scale production of B-exportables that the external or other economies of scale begin to operate (e.g. the greater or smaller labour force leads to a better or smaller dispersion of skill) and the cost of A-exportables falls and that of B-exportables rises. In such a case a chance shift of production from A-exportables to B-exportables in A combined with a chance shift in the opposite direction in B might in the short run set into motion forces restoring the previous equilibrium and these forces might themselves operate effectively with only a small time-lag, so that the previous equilibrium Q_3 would in fact be restored before the destabilizing influence of economies of scale had become effective.

In the case of Figure XVIII exactly the same arguments apply to the equilibrium point Q_3 where both countries are producing both commodities. The position of equilibrium is essentially an unstable one, though it might have a precarious stability if the development of economies of scale was a very delayed result of any change in production. But, although country A still produces something of both commodities, the same destabilizing influences are not at work in the case of positions Q_1 and Q_2, because at these points B is specializing completely. Thus if we start at the point Q_1, it is impossible for there to be a chance increase in the production of A-exportables and decrease in that of B-exportables in A, combined with a chance decrease in the production of A-exportables and increase in the production of B-exportables in B, for the very simple reason that in B the production of A-exportables is already reduced to zero and the production of B-exportables is already expanded to its maximum possible level. If there were a chance increase in the production of A-exportables and decrease in the production of B-exportables in A, this would cause an increase in the world supply of the former and a decrease in the world supply of the latter; and the price, as well as the marginal cost, of producing A-exportables would fall.

Starting from Q_1 in Figure XVIII, it is, of course, not physically impossible for B to start to produce A-exportables. Thus it is possible for a chance decrease in the production of A-exportables and an increase in the production of B-exportables in A to be combined with an increase in the production of A-exportables and decrease in the production of B-exportables in B, on such a scale that the world demand prices for the two products remain more or less unchanged. Producers in A would then have an increased incentive to produce still less of A-exportables (whose marginal cost would have risen because of the decreased scale of production) and to produce still more of B-exportables. But now it would no longer be true that producers in B would have a cumulative incentive to expand the production of A-exportables. On the contrary at the equilibrium point Q_1 a zero amount of A-exportables is being produced because the marginal cost of producing the first unit is greatly in excess of the demand price. The production of a small amount of A-exportables in B can, therefore, only be undertaken at a serious loss. If it were by chance started, it would soon be stopped. In effect, therefore, a chance decrease in the production of A-exportables in A at the point Q_1 will involve a reduction in the world supply and a rise in the price of A-exportables; and this change in the price relationship will help to restore the previous equilibrium.

We may conclude, therefore, that the local optimum points Q_1 and Q_2 in Figures XVII and XVIII are stable, and that the pessimum point Q_3, at which both countries produce both commodities, is essentially unstable, though time-lags in adjustment might be such as to stabilize it. Let us conclude this chapter by considering the desirability of the possible points of stable equilibrium from the point of view of both countries. From the trade-indifference curves in Figure XVII it can be seen that, as they are there drawn, Q_1 is the best point for both countries. It lies on the two trade-indifference curves marked B_1 and A_1. Q_2 is the next best position for both countries, lying on the trade-indifference curves A_2 and B_2. Q_3 is the worst position for both countries, lying on A_3 and B_3. Yet Q_1 and Q_2 at least may both be positions of stable equilibrium; and it might require some structural jolt to move the economy from Q_2 to Q_1.

Of course, it is only one special case that Q_1 should be better than Q_2 for both countries. The A-trade-indifference curves could be so redrawn that A_2 after going through Q_2 passed above instead of below Q_1, in which case to avoid intersection of trade-indifference curves A_1 after passing through Q_1 would pass below Q_2. If the B-trade-indifference curves remained as drawn, then Q_1 would be the better position for B but Q_2 the better position for A. We may conclude, therefore, that in the case of important increasing returns to scale in both countries a structural jolt might be able to shift the world economy from one position of stable equilibrium (in which one country specialized wholly on one line of product) to a second position of stable equilibrium (in which that country specialized wholly on the other line of product), and that such a change might be better for both countries, worse for both, or better for one and worse for the other.

In this and the previous chapter we have considered cases of constant and decreasing costs. This was in the nature of a digression. We shall now for the rest of our study revert to the assumption of increasing costs, leaving it to the reader, with the help of these two chapters, to apply the following arguments to the cases of constant and decreasing costs, if he so wishes.

CHAPTER VI

The Representation of Commercial Policy with a Zero Balance of Trade

WE revert, then, to the assumption of increasing costs; and we continue to assume that there is no deficit or surplus on the balance of trade. But we now modify the assumption that there is free trade in both countries. There are eight "simple" forms of commercial policy to be considered:—

Import duty in A	Import subsidy in A
Export duty in B	Export subsidy in B
Import duty in B	Import subsidy in B
Export duty in A	Export subsidy in A

There are in addition a very large number of "complex" forms of commercial policy interventions, such as import duties in both A and B combined, perhaps, with export subsidies in one or both countries.

I

PROFESSOR LERNER'S SOLUTION

Let us first consider the geometrical representation of the left-hand four of the above simple commercial policy combinations which Professor Lerner gave in his article on "The Symmetry between Import and Export Taxes" in *Economica* for August 1936. This is illustrated in Figure XIX, the only difference between our Figure XIX and the figures in Professor Lerner's article being that our figure also shows the production and consumption points inside each country when we assume that each country produces something of both commodities in conditions of increasing cost.

(i) *An Import Duty in A*

Let us suppose that the government in country A imposes an import duty with the *ad valorem* rate of $\dfrac{Q_aK}{JK}$ (Figure XIX). For an amount OJ of B-exportables, consumers in A will pay JQ_a (so that $\dfrac{JQ_a}{JO}$ or the slope of α represents the market price relationship in A). But KQ_a out of JQ_a will accrue to the government in A so that producers in B will receive only JK (so that $\dfrac{JK}{JO}$ or the slope of β represents the market price relationship in B). For any slope β (i.e. any market price relationship in B) we must accordingly draw a corresponding α-price line such that $\dfrac{Q_aK}{JK}$ equals the given *ad valorem* rate of import duty. We can rotate the pencil $\beta O\alpha$ around on its point O, always keeping the above relationship between the slopes of α and β. For every point Q_b at which the β-line cuts B's ordinary offer curve O_b, there will be a corresponding point Q_a where the α-line cuts A's offer curve O_a. Professor Lerner points out that equilibrium will be reached at a value of the slopes of β and so of α at which the government in A is prepared to spend its revenue (KQ_a) on B-exportables and A-exportables in the ratio $\dfrac{KL}{LQ_a}$. This means that the government in A directly consumes LQ_a of A-exportables and spends the remainder of its revenue (KL), at the untaxed price line β, on LQ_b of B-exportables.

That this is a position of full equilibrium can be shown in the following way. Place A's production block with its corner at Q_a and B's production block with its corner at Q_b. Since Q_a is on A's offer curve the price line α will be tangential at Q_a to an A-trade-indifference curve

(I_{ia}) ; and because of the relationship between trade- and consumption-indifference curves, there will be a corresponding A-consumption-indifference curve tangential to A's production block at M, the slope of which (α_1) will be the same as that of the price line α. Extend α_1 to H and vertically below M at the base of A's production block (at N), draw α_2 with the same slope and extend to G. Similarly from B's production block derive the points S, R, E, and F, and the two price lines β_1 and β_2 with the same slope as β.

Now the income of the factors of production in A in terms of A-exportables is OH, OG which is equal to NQ_a representing the income from the production in A of A-exportables, and HG which measures the value of MN at the price line α representing the value in A-exportables of the output in A of B-exportables. Consumers in A with the income HO move up the price line α_1 to their highest consumption-indifference curve at M. Thus private consumers in A need to import OJ of B-exportables in order to supplement their home production and they leave JQ_a of the home production of A-exportables over for export to B or for purchase by A's government.

If A's government, out of the revenue from the import duty, purchases Q_bL of B-exportables, then imports of OJ + Q_bL, i.e. of Q_bD, will be required by A; and if A's government consumes LQ_a of A-exportables only JL or OD will be available for export to B. But if B exports DQ_b and imports OD, then B's production block with its corner at Q_b gives at S the actual consumption point which must rule in B. And by a similar process of reasoning by which it was shown that in A total consumers' income would be OH and the equilibrium consumption point at M, it can be shown that in B total consumers' income will be OE and the equilibrium consumption point will in fact be S. Measured in units of B-exportables consumers in B will have an income of OE (i.e. OF or Q_bR from the production of B-exportables and FE or RS converted at the price β from the production of A-exportables). They will move up the price line β_1 to S. Because of the nature of the offer curve, there will be a B-trade-indifference curve I_{tb} with the slope β at Q_b; and because of the relationship between the B-trade-indifference curve and the B-consumption-indifference curve the line β_1, which has the same slope as β, will be tangential to B's production block at the point S at which a B-consumption-indifference curve is also tangential to the production block.

In what follows we shall refer to four different price relationships: First, the market price relationship in A is the ratio between the price of the two products in the free consumers' and producers' market in A. This is shown by the slope of α, α_1, or α_2.

Second, the similar market price relationship in B is shown by β, β_1, or β_2. Since we are dealing with a case of protection in A's market, the price of B-exportables in terms of A-exportables is higher in A than in B, i.e. the slope of α is less than that of β.

Third, the barter terms of trade* show the amount of B-exportables which are obtained from B per unit of A-exportables sent to B. In our present case it is represented by the slope of β.

Fourth, for certain purposes we may wish to talk of the monetary rate of exchange. We assume monetary policies in A and B which stabilize the factor-cost price of A-exportables in terms of A's currency and of B-exportables in terms of B's currency. The rate of exchange is thus the ratio between the untaxed-unsubsidized price of B-exportables in B and the untaxed-unsubsidized price of A-exportables in A. In the case of an import duty in A

---

* Since we are still dealing with the case of a zero balance of trade we need not distinguish between the net barter terms of trade and the gross barter terms of trade. But we shall have to make this additional distinction between various exchange ratios in later sections.

this is the same as the barter terms of trade and the market price relationship in B. In other words in our present case the rate of exchange is also measured by β.

(ii) *An Export Duty in B*

We can regard an export duty in B as being exactly the same thing as an import duty in A, the revenue from which is handed over by the government of A to the government of B. In both cases B-exportables are taxed as they pass from B to A; the only difference is that in the case of the import duty in A the revenue accrues to A's government and in the case of the export duty in B it accrues to B's government.

If, then, the government of B is prepared to spend the revenue (KQ_a) which it receives as to LQ_a on the purchase of LQ_a of A-exportables and as to KL on the purchase of Q_bL of B-exportables, the position in Figure XIX will equally well represent the case of an export duty in B. The only difference is that the revenue Q_bL of B-exportables and LQ_a of A-exportables is now consumed by B's government. To this extent, of course, the barter terms of trade are turned against A. The taxed, instead of the untaxed, price of B-exportables is what country A as a whole has to pay for the import of a unit of B-exportables. The barter terms of trade are, therefore, represented by α (the market price ratio in A) instead of β (the market price ratio in B). But β still represents the rate of exchange between B's and A's currency.

(iii) *An Import Duty in B*

By an exactly similar process of reasoning as that which was employed under (i), but with the substitution of country A for country B and vice versa, it can be shown that Figure XIX represents the effect of the imposition of an import duty in B at the *ad valorem* rate of $\dfrac{Q_bC}{CD}$.

If the government of B is prepared to spend Q_bL of this revenue directly on B-exportables and CL, at the untaxed price α of A-exportables, on the purchase of LQ_a of A-exportables, then Q_bL and Q_aL will represent the proceeds of the import duty which are consumed by B's government; β will represent the market price relationship in B; and α will represent the market price relationship in A, the barter terms of trade, and the rate of exchange.

Now it can easily be seen that in Figure XIX $\dfrac{Q_aK}{JK} = \dfrac{Q_bC}{CD}$. This can be shown as follows. The two triangles OJK and UKQ_a have all angles equal, so that $\dfrac{Q_aK}{JK} = \dfrac{UQ_a}{JO} = \dfrac{UQ_a}{Q_aV}$. But $\dfrac{UQ_a}{Q_aV} = \dfrac{Q_bC}{CD}$, so that $\dfrac{Q_aK}{JK} = \dfrac{Q_bC}{CD}$. But we have already shown under (ii) that Figure XIX represents the case of an export duty of $\dfrac{KQ_a}{JK}$ in B, where the revenue $Q_bL + LQ_a$ accrues to the government of B. But, as we have just seen, it also represents the case of an import duty in B of the same *ad valorem* incidence, $\dfrac{Q_bC}{CD}$, where the same proceeds of the revenue $Q_bL + LQ_a$ accrue to the government of B.

In other words it makes no *real* difference whether the government of B taxes trade by means of a given *ad valorem* import duty or by means of the same *ad valorem* export duty, provided that in both cases it elects to divide the revenue in the same way on purchases of the two commodities.

But the choice between import duties and export

duties does, of course, make a great difference to the monetary mechanism of adjustment. With the import duty in B, α will measure the rate of exchange between the two currencies; in return for imports of OD of A-exportables (with a fixed price in terms of A's currency) importers in B would have to give only CD of their currency to purchase OD of A's currency; the remaining part of the price, $Q_b C$, would be the tax which they would have to pay to their own government. With the export duty in B, β will measure the rate of exchange between the two currencies; in return for imports of OD of A-exportables, importers in B would have to pay $Q_b D$ in their own currency to purchase OD-worth of A's currency; but of this amount of B's currency ($Q_b D$) a part, namely $Q_b C$, would be taken away by the taxing authority in B, when it was spent by A's importers in purchasing only CD of B-exportables for export from B. This conforms with the well-known and common-sense conclusion that if a government (B) removed an import duty and imposed an export tax, this would cause the foreign exchange value of B's currency to depreciate, provided that the domestic price of A's main products was stabilized in terms of A's currency and that of B's main products in terms of B's currency. The increased demand for imports in B and the reduced incentive to export due to the tax changes would increase the demand in B for A's currency, and B's currency would depreciate. But there is, of course, no reason to believe that the barter terms of trade will move against B, because while the movement of the exchange rate against B will tend to make B's products cheaper relatively to A's, the imposition of the export duty on B's products will raise the price at which B's products exchange for A's. Indeed the above analysis shows that if full employment is maintained and if the government of B spends the revenue of the export duty in just the same way as it would have spent the revenue of the import duty, and if the *ad valorem* incidence of the export duty is the same as that of the import duty which it replaces, the barter terms of trade and all other real factors will be unchanged as between the two positions.

(iv) *An Export Duty in A*

The import duty in B can be turned into an export duty in A merely by handing the revenue over for expenditure by the government in A. In this case in Figure XIX $\dfrac{Q_b C}{CD}$ represents the rate of export duty in A; $Q_b L + Q_a L$ represents the use of the proceeds of the duty by the government of A; α represents the market price relationship in α and the rate of exchange; and β represents the market price relationship in B and the barter terms of trade. It will be seen that this is exactly the same result as the import duty in A (case (i)) except that the rate of exchange is now represented by α instead of by β.

2

THE PROBLEM OF SUBSIDIES

It will be seen that Professor Lerner's geometrical representation of commercial policy which we have just discussed does not cover the case of subsidies. It is, however, possible logically to extend the method of his analysis to cover the case of subsidies, and this is done in Figure XX. But it will become clear that this involves one major difficulty for realistic interpretation.

Any subsidy to trade whether on imports or on exports and whether paid by A's government or by B's government will tend to make the ratio of the market price of A-exportables to that of B-exportables higher in A than in B. If A's government pays an export subsidy this will tend to raise the market or unsubsidized price of A-exportables in terms of B-exportables in A (as more of A-exportables are produced and their price goes up) and to lower the market or subsidized price of A-exportables in terms of B-exportables in B (as more A-exportables are put on B's market by A); if A's government subsidizes imports, this will tend to lower the market or subsidized price of B-exportables in A's market and to raise the market or unsubsidized price of B-exportables in B as the increased demand for them raises their cost of production; similarly if B's government subsidizes exports, this will lower the market or subsidized price of B-exportables in A and will raise their market or unsubsidized price in B; and finally if B's government subsidizes imports this will lower the market or subsidized price of A-exportables in B and will raise the market or unsubsidized price of A-exportables in A. In other words with subsidies to trade the α-price line (the market price in A) will always be steeper than the β-price line (the market price in B), as is shown in Figure XX. This is the opposite to Figure XIX, the case of taxes on trade where the β-line is steeper than the α line.

Figure XX represents the case where a subsidy to trade of the *ad valorem* rate of $\dfrac{Q_bC}{Q_bD}$ is paid on imports or exports by A's or B's government.* We may briefly enumerate the meaning of the diagram in each of the four possible cases.

(i) *An Import Subsidy in A*

The price line β represents the market price relationship in B, the barter terms of trade, and the rate of exchange. At this price relationship private traders in

* For the reasons given on page 49 above $\dfrac{Q_bC}{Q_bD} = \dfrac{Q_aK}{Q_aJ}$, which can equally well be taken as measuring the rate of subsidy.

B export OD of B-exportables and import in return DQ_b of A-exportables. But on B's exports of B-exportables A's government pays a subsidy of CQ_b, so that A's consumers can consume and A's producers can produce at a price relationship α. A's importers therefore purchase OJ in excess of A's home production of B-exportables and her exporters export only JQ_a out of her home production of A-exportables. The private market is, therefore, short of Q_aL of A-exportables and Q_bL of B-exportables. These amounts are, however, produced by A's government like a rabbit out of the conjurer's hat to pay the import subsidy; and there will be full equilibrium if A's government elects to raise the monetary funds to pay the import subsidy as to a proportion $\dfrac{CL}{CQ_b}$ by producing A-exportables out of the conjurer's hat and selling them on the market and as to $\dfrac{LQ_b}{CQ_b}$ by producing B-exportables out of the hat and selling them on the market.

(ii) *An Export Subsidy in B*

This is just the same as (i) except that the government of B now has to produce the revenue for the subsidy. The price line β still measures the market price relationship in B and the rate of exchange; but α, the market price relationship in A, now represents the barter terms of trade. In this case LQ_b of B-exportables and LQ_a of A-exportables are produced out of thin air by B's government and are handed over to traders in A as a subsidy together with the B-exportables Q_bD which B's private exporters are supplying at the market price line β.

(iii) *An Import Subsidy in B*

The price line β represents the market price in B; but the price line α represents the market price in A, the barter terms of trade, and the rate of exchange. Private traders in A offer, at the market price α, JQ_a of A-exportables or of A's currency for JO of B-exportables or B's currency. To these imports the government of B adds a subsidy at the rate of $\dfrac{Q_bC}{Q_bD}$, the revenue for which it produces by providing Q_aL of A-exportables and Q_bL of B-exportables out of thin air. At the favourable subsidized rate of β, B traders are willing to trade at Q_b which, with the subsidies, just clears the market.

(iv) *An Export Subsidy in A*

This is just the same as the preceding case except that it is now the government of A which must finance the subsidies by producing the extra supplies $Q_aL + Q_bL$. α still represents the market price in A, and the rate of exchange; but β, the market relationship in B, now represents the barter terms of trade, because for an export of B-exportables of Q_bD country B receives an import of A-exportables of OD. The subsidy $Q_aL + Q_bL$ is now created out of thin air by A's government to supplement the revenue (Q_bD) which A-exporters receive for their exports (OD).

It is now easy to see why Professor Lerner's method cannot really be applied to the problem of subsidies to trade. While it was quite reasonable to assume in the case of duties on trade that the additional revenue of the State ($Q_aL + Q_bL$ of Figure XIX) was absorbed in certain arbitrary proportions in government consumption outside the market, it is absurd to assume that in the case of subsidies the additional expenditure of the State ($Q_aL + Q_bL$ of Figure XX) is financed in certain arbitrary proportions by government production outside the market. Governments can consume additionally outside the consumers' market but they cannot produce additional quantities outside the normal production system. We must seek some other method of representation if we want to depict subsidies as well as duties.

3

ANOTHER METHOD OF REPRESENTATION, ILLUSTRATED BY THE PROBLEM OF STATE TRADING

The missing link is not far to seek. When subsidies on international trade are paid out we must assume that the funds for the additional governmental subsidies are raised by some other form of taxation. We shall assume this to take the form of a general proportionate rate of tax on all incomes earned in the country concerned.

We can make an analogous assumption about the use which the State makes of any revenue which is raised by the imposition of taxes on international trade. We can assume that, instead of using the revenue to make arbitrarily predetermined purchases of A-exportables and B-exportables for its own consumption, it uses the funds to pay a general proportionate rate of subsidy to all incomes.* The advantage of this method is not merely that we can treat subsidies as easily as taxes, but also that we need not introduce an arbitrary assumption about the use of State revenue from trade taxes; we can allow the ordinary consumption-indifference map of the citizens to take care of the use of the additional revenue as between A-exportables and B-exportables.

Consider any point such as Q in Figures XXI and XXII, which is assumed to be on B's offer curve but not on A's offer curve. Since Q is on B's offer curve at the price line β traders in B will be prepared to export

---

* In fact it might well use the funds to reduce an existing rate of income tax. This is essentially the system which we are going to adopt except that, as we have no public finance except that which is involved in taxes and subsidies on international trade, we have no income tax to start with, and must, therefore, pay an income subsidy instead of reducing an existing rate of income tax.

55

CQ in return for OC. Draw the price line α through the point Q, tangential to the A-trade-indifference curve which passes through Q. Since Q is not on A's offer curve the price line α will not pass through the origin O. We suppose in Figure XXI that it cuts the X-axis to the left of O and in Figure XXII that it cuts the X-axis to the right of O. Place A's production block in position with its corner at Q. Draw the price line α_1 at the point of tangency (G) of A's production block with an A-consumption-indifference curve; α_1 will be parallel to α. Draw also the price line α_2 with the same slope through the point H on the base of A's production block vertically below G.

Then in both figures α, α_1, and α_2 will represent the market price line in A. It follows that FD in both figures will represent the value of the national income at factor cost in A, measured in terms of A-exportables, ED being the value of the output in A of A-exportables and FE being the value of the output in A of B-exportables converted into terms of A-exportables at the market price line α. But while FD in both Figures measures the value of the net national income in A, the point G will represent an equilibrium consumption point for A's consumers only if FO and not FD represents the total amount of purchasing power which final buyers in A have available to spend on the two commodities. If final buyers in A do have FO to spend, they will move up the price line α_1 to G which only in these conditions will represent an internal consumption equilibrium in A. And in this case Q will also represent a trade equilibrium point for A's producers and consumers. HQ of A-exportables is produced in A, but only HJ is consumed, so that JQ is left for export. And GH + JO of B-exportables is consumed in A, but only GH is produced, so that JO is imported.

We can, therefore, lay down the following proposition

which we shall use extensively throughout the remainder of this book. Take any point Q in the trade quadrant XOY. Through Q draw the price line α which is tangential to the A-trade-indifference curve which passes through Q, and let the line α cut the X-axis at D. Then Q will represent a point of trade equilibrium for A's producers and consumers if the purchasing power in the hands of A's final buyers is equal to A's net national income plus (or minus) an amount measured by the extent to which the point D is to the left (or to the right) of the origin O. When we come to examine the geometrical representation of a deficit (or surplus) on the balance of trade we shall find that this may be a reason why D falls to the left (or the right) of O; and in this case the domestic purchasing power provided by the national income is supplemented by the amount borrowed from abroad (or is reduced by the amount lent abroad). But another reason why domestic purchasing power may exceed (or fall short of) the net national income is because of the income subsidy (or income tax) which is made possible by the revenue raised from trade taxation (or necessitated by the public expenditure involved in trade subsidies).

It is possible to express these propositions in terms of national-income national-expenditure accounts. The distance FD in Figures XXI and XXII measures the net national income at factor cost in country A, i.e. the value in A in terms of A's exportables of the total output of A-exportables and B-exportables. But FO measures the domestic expenditure at market prices measured in terms of A-exportables. There are two reasons why domestic expenditure at market prices may exceed net national income at factor cost. The first is a balance-of-trade deficit. In this case the goods and services to be purchased on A's market exceed the goods and services produced on A's market by the excess of imports over

57

exports. The second is a trade tax. The funds available to be spent at market prices on goods and services in A will exceed the earnings of A's factors of production because of the State revenue from import or export duties which is available to supplement purchases made out of earnings.

The first of these two reasons will be the subject matter of Chapter VII below. Our present concern is with the divergences between net national income at factor cost and domestic expenditure at market prices which are due to indirect taxes and subsidies.

Let us turn, then, to the way in which Figures XXI and XXII may be used to represent commercial policy. In both figures QC will represent the amount of B-exportables imported into A and OC the amount of A-exportables imported into B, and β will therefore represent the barter terms of trade. Now it is easy to show that in Figure XXI $\frac{DO}{OC}$ will represent the *ad valorem* rate of trade tax which will be required in A to make traders in A ready to trade at the point Q, and that DO will represent the total revenue raised from trade taxes and used to subsidize incomes in A. Similarly, $\frac{DO}{OC}$ in Figure XXII will represent the *ad valorem* rate of trade subsidy required to make traders in A trade at the point Q, and DO will represent the total expenditure by A's government on trade subsidies and the total taxation on income needed to finance the subsidies.

Consider first the case of trade taxes in Figure XXI. Consumers in A have a total spendable income of FO, FD from their earnings, and DO from the governmental subsidies to income. They move up the price line α_1 to G. In this position they are offering DC (at the price line α) for the amount (QC) of B-exportables which has to be purchased from B. But of the market price DC offered in A for B-exportables, the government in A takes DO away in taxation, leaving only CO for the traders in B. But since Q is on B's offer curve the exchange of CO for QC leaves B's traders in equilibrium.

$\frac{DO}{OC}$ can represent a rate of import duty or of export duty in A. If it is an import duty, then OC of A's money is offered by A's traders for CQ of B's money, but A's traders have also to pay DO of A's money to A's government in import duty in order to be allowed to change the CQ of B's money into an import of B's products into A. In this case β is the rate of exchange as well as the barter terms of trade. If the trade tax is an export tax, then A's traders offer DC of A's money to purchase CQ of B's money which they can then change into B's products and import into A free of tax. But when B's importers use the DC of A's money so acquired to purchase A's products for export to B, they have to pay an export duty of DO and are thus left with only OC of A's money for the purchase of OC of A's products. α is now the rate of exchange, though β still measures the barter terms of trade.

We turn next to Figure XXII and the case of a trade subsidy. Consumers in A have FO to spend, FD being their earnings but OD being taken away in income tax. They move up the price line α_1 to G. In this position they are offering DC (at the price line α) for QC of imports of B-exportables. But to this market price of DC offered in A for B-exportables from B the government in A adds OD in subsidies, thus providing OC for the traders in B.

$\frac{DO}{OC}$ can represent a rate of import or of export subsidy in A. If it is an import subsidy then OC of A's money is offered by A's traders to obtain CQ of B's money, and β is the rate of exchange. But when A's traders actually

59

import CQ of B's products they receive back a subsidy from the government, equal to OD of the price previously paid for the foreign exchange necessary to purchase the imports, the net price being only DC. If the subsidy is on exports, then A's importers pay DC only for CQ of B's money or of B's products which are now imported without subsidy. In this case α will represent the rate of exchange. But when B's traders use the DC of A's money to purchase A's products they have OD added to them in the form of a subsidy by A's government, so that they receive OC of A's products for the CQ of B's money and so of B's products which they have surrendered.

Now we can, of course, make an exactly similar construction for country B. For this purpose we place B's production block with its corner Q at some position in the trade quadrant YOX, not on B's offer curve, as in Figure XXIII. Draw the line β through Q tangential to the B-trade-indifference curve at Q. Let it cut YY' at K. If K is below O, then a trade tax and an income subsidy of OK is needed in B; if K is above O, a trade subsidy and an income tax of OK is required.

In Figure XXIII we also put together these constructions for both countries. For this purpose put country A's and country B's production blocks corner to corner, and let the point Q rest, as in Figure XXIII, on some point in the quadrant YOX which is neither on A's nor on B's offer curve. Complete the construction as explained above for both A and B. The line γ which runs through O and Q will measure the real terms of trade since OC of A's products are exchanged for QC of B's. Consumers in A have earnings of FD and an income subsidy of DO; they use their spendable income of FO by moving up the price line α_1 to G. They import QC and pay DC for it; but of this DO is paid in a trade tax and used by the government of A to finance

the income subsidies in A. Traders in B receive only
OC of A's products. Consumers in B have KM earnings
plus KO income subsidies to spend. They move up the
price line β_1 to N. They import OC and offer JK in
exchange; but of this OK is taken in tax by the government of B and used to pay the income subsidies in B.
Traders in A receive only OJ.

It is to be observed that in Figures XXI, XXII,
and XXIII we have not succeeded in showing how the
trading point Q will be determined by trade taxes or
subsidies of a given level in A and B. We have done
the opposite. We have shown what levels of trade taxes
or subsidies will be required in A and B in order to
cause a given trading point Q to represent an equilibrium
position. The former problem, which we have not really
tackled but to which we shall return in the following
section, is really the problem of tariffs and subsidies:
given certain rates of tax or subsidies, what will happen
to trade? The latter problem, which we claim to have
solved, is really that of State trading: given a certain
fixed barter (OC for CQ) between the two countries,
what price and income relationships must occur within
the two economies to make that barter deal acceptable
in the market?

We can, therefore, interpret Figure XXIII in this way.
The point Q represents a deal between the State trading
monopolies of A and B, OC of A-exportables to be
exchanged for CQ of B-exportables. The State import
monopoly puts the imports CQ on to the market in A
for sale. They are restricted in amount and fetch the
high price represented by the slope of α. A's State-
trading monopoly receives DC for them, but has to pay
over to B's State-trading monopoly only OC. DO represents the profit margin of A's State-trading monopoly,
the revenue from which is used to pay income subsidies
in A.

At the same time B's State-trading monopoly is importing OC. This limited import fetches the high price of β when sold in B's market. B's monopoly receives JK for it, but pays only JO to A's monopoly. OK is the profit margin of B's monopoly, the revenue from which is used to pay income subsidies in B.

If D had lain to the right of O (as in Figure XXII), this would have represented a loss of A's State-trading monopoly. The relatively abundant imports QC now fetch only the low price of DC, though OC is to be paid to B's monopoly. The State-trading monopoly makes a loss of OD (i.e. subsidizes trade by OD), which is financed by raising an equivalent income tax in A. And similarly in B, if K (in Figure XXIII) had been above O.

We have just observed that Figure XXIII shows only the case in which Q is in such a position—i.e. is a point of such restricted trade—that it needs trade taxes or State-trading profits in both countries to clear the market. But this is not, of course, necessarily the case. There are in all six possible conditions which it is useful to consider. These are shown schematically in Table I.

Case 1 is that actually shown in Figure XXIII. There are trade taxes or State-trading profits in both countries. The tax or profit margin on imports into A will raise the market price of B-exportables in A and the tax or profit margin on imports into B will raise the market price of A-exportables in B. For both these reasons the price of B-exportables is high in A relatively to its height in B; β is necessarily steeper than α, as can be seen from Figure XXIII.

In case 2 of Table I the trade tax or profit margin in B gives place to a trade subsidy or margin of loss. K rises along the Y-axis above O. But it is still below R, and β is still steeper than α. This means that while the trade or profit margin in A tends to raise the market price of B-exportables in A, the trade subsidy or loss in B

TABLE I

Trade Tax or State-trading Profit in A	Trade Tax or State-trading Profit in B (K below O)	β steeper than α (R above K) (1)
(D to the left of O)	Trade Subsidy or State-trading Loss in B (K above O)	β steeper than α (R above K) (2)
		α steeper than β (R below K) (3)
Trade Subsidy or State-trading Loss in A	Trade Tax or State-trading Profit in B (K below O)	β steeper than α (R above K) (4)
(D to the right of O)		α steeper than β (R below K) (5)
	Trade Subsidy or State-trading Loss in A (K above O)	α steeper than β (R below K) (6)

tends to lower the market price of B-exportables in A. But the former influence still outweighs the latter. But in case 3 the trade subsidy or loss in B has become so important relatively to the trade tax or profit in A that K rises above R, and α is steeper than β. The effect of B's trade subsidy or loss in lowering the market price of B-exportables in A has more influence than the effect of A's trade tax or profit in raising this market price.

It is of some interest to map out the trade quadrant YOX into the six divisions shown in Table I.* This is done in Figures XXIV, XXV, XXVI, and XXVII.

From Figure XXIV it can be seen that at any point to the left of A's offer curve O_a the tangent to the A-trade-indifference curve will cut the X-axis to the left of the origin; and a trade tax or profit will be required to maintain equilibrium in the market. This can be proved as follows. Consider any such point C. Draw the line OC and extend till it cuts the offer curve at G; and call this line α_0. Draw the A-trade-indifference curve which is tangential to α_0 at G, and let D represent the point on this indifference curve which is vertically above C. If the A-trade-indifference curve which passes through C were as steeply sloped as α_0, then it would cut the A-trade-indifference curve which passes through D at some point between D and G. Since trade-indifference curves do not intersect, the slope α_1 of the trade-indifference curve which passes through C is less steep than α_0, so that α_1 will pass to the left of O cutting XX' at H.

It can similarly be shown that at any point to the right of A's offer curve the tangent to the A-indifference curve will cut the X-axis to the right of the origin; and a trade subsidy or loss will be needed to clear the market. In Figure XXIV E is such a point. The trade-indifference curve which passes through E must have a steeper

* Dr. Helen Makower has suggested to me much of the following argument.

slope (α_2) than α_0 to prevent this trade-indifference curve from cutting the trade-indifference curve which passes through G, so that J lies to the right of O.

It can similarly be shown that at any point lying below B's offer curve the slope of the B-trade-indifference curve is such that its tangent will cut the Y-axis below the origin, representing a trade tax or profit; and at any point above B's offer curve it will cut the Y-axis above the origin, representing a trade subsidy or loss. These conclusions serve to map out the areas of the quadrant YOX which are relevant to the first two columns of Table I.

Figure XXV illustrates the considerations which are relevant to the last column of Table I. The quadrant YOX is closely packed with A- and B-trade-indifference curves. We may name the locus K-K' of the points of tangency between A- and B-trade-indifference-curves the "contract curve." It is intuitively obvious from a consideration of the point C in Figure XXV that at any point to the South-West of K-K' the α-line will be less steep than the β-line. And from the point D it can be seen that at any point North-East of K-K' the α-line is steeper than the β-line. K-K' is the locus of the points at which the α-line and β-line have the same slope.

In Figures XXVI and XXVII we put the considerations of Figures XXIV and XXV together. Figure XXVI is the normal case where the two offer curves cut only once, i.e. at a point at which the sum of the price elasticities of demand for imports in the two countries is greater than unity.* The area marked (1) being to the left of A's offer curve represents a position of trade tax or profit in A, and being below B's offer curve represents a position of trade tax or profit in B as well. It therefore corresponds to row 1 in column 3 of Table I. The area marked (2), being to the left of A's offer curve

* For an explanation of this point see pp. 87–90 below.

E

represents a position of trade profit or tax in A; being above B's offer curve it represents a position of trade subsidy or loss in B; and being to the South-West of the contract curve it represents a position in which the β-line is steeper than the α-line. It therefore maps out the area corresponding to row 2 in Table I. And so on for the areas (3), (4), (5), and (6).

Figure XXVII maps out these same areas in the case in which the offer curves cut more than once. In the case shown they cut three times at C, D, and E, the intersections at C and E being stable points at which the sum of the price elasticities of demand for imports in the two countries is greater than one and the middle intersection at D being at a position of unstable equilibrium at which the sum of the two elasticities is less than one.* The map is the same as in Figure XXVI in its main features except for the small islands of areas (2) and (3) between C and D, and of areas (4) and (5) between D and E. Consider the island marked (5) between D and E. It is to the right of O_a, and therefore represents a position of trade subsidy or loss in A; it is below O_b and therefore represents a position of trade tax or profit in B; and it is to the North and East of K-K' and therefore represents a position in which the α-line is steeper than the β-line. From Table I it can be seen that it is, therefore, correctly labelled (5).

We can, therefore, choose any point Q in the trade quadrant YOX; and according to its position on this map we can say what will be the price and income relationship in A and B needed to clear the market with the given amounts of imports and exports.

Before we leave this topic it may be of interest to make one comment on the position which arises if a trade profit is needed in one country and a trade loss in the other. Figure XXVIII represents the case in which Q

* See pp. 91–92 below.

lies on the contract curve so that the α-line coincides with the β-line. They cut the Y-axis at F and the X-axis at D. According to the preceding analysis this represents a position in which γ represents the net and the gross barter terms of trade between A and B. But in A a trade tax is imposed at the rate of $\dfrac{DO}{OC}$. DC is paid by consumers in A for QC of imports; but DO of this is taken in revenue and used to subsidize incomes in A. Only OC is paid to traders in B. In B consumers pay EF for imports of EQ; but the government in B subsidizes this with OF and raises the money for the subsidy by income taxation of OF.

But exactly the same position could be brought about without any trade taxes in A or trade subsidies in B. Suppose that the government in B raised OF in income taxes in B and paid this over to the government in A which used it to pay income subsidies of OF (or DO at the price line $\alpha\beta$) in A. Then $\alpha\beta$ would represent the equilibrium net barter terms of trade, though γ would, of course, still represent the gross barter terms of trade. The gross terms would be more favourable to A than the net barter terms because of the free gift of some goods from B to A. Citizens of A would have OD plus their earnings to spend at a price relationship $\alpha\beta$; and citizens in B would have their earnings minus OF to spend at the same price relationship $\alpha\beta$. Q would then be the resultant position of trade equilibrium.

From this we can deduce the important conclusion that when trade is taxed in one country and subsidized in another, then—to the extent that the subsidies and taxes amount to the same total—this is exactly equivalent in real terms to a direct transfer of purchasing power of the same amount from the citizens of the country in which trade is subsidized (or conducted at a loss) to the citizens of the country in which trade is taxed (or run at a profit).

Figure XXVIII showed the case where the total trade subsidies in B were exactly equal to the total trade taxes in A. In Figure XXIX we show the case where the trade subsidies in B are less than the trade profits in A. This Figure might show the case where

(i) the net and gross barter terms of trade are γ,

(ii) DO measures the trade tax and income subsidy in A, and

(iii) OF measures the trade subsidy and income tax in B.

But Figure XXIX could equally well depict the case in which

(i) the gross barter terms of trade are γ,

(ii) the net barter terms of trade are β,

(iii) OF measures the income tax in B,

(iv) DG measures the trade tax in A, and

(v) DO measures the income subsidy in A, DG being financed from the proceeds of the trade tax in A and GO from the proceeds of the gift of OF from the government of B to the government of A.

4

THE TAXED AND SUBSIDIZED OFFER CURVES

We can turn now to the problem of deriving the trade point Q when the rates of import and export tax in A and B are given.

In Figure XXX draw a horizontal line $C_1 C_6$ above the OX axis, and let it cut successive A-trade-indifference curves at the points C_1, C_2, C_3, C_4, C_5, and C_6. Of these points C_1 lies on the OY axis, and C_4 lies on A's offer curve because the tangent to the A-trade-indifference curve at C_4 goes through the origin O. Draw α_1, α_2, etc., tangential to the A-trade-indifference curves at C_1, C_2, etc., and let these lines cut the X-axis at E_1, E_2, etc.

Drop perpendiculars from C_1, C_2, etc., on to the X-axis to cut it at D_1, D_2, etc.

Consider the point C_3. In order that A-consumers should be willing to trade at this point, as we have already seen, α_3 must represent the market price relationship in A, a trade tax must be imposed at the rate of $\dfrac{E_3O}{OD_3}$, and E_3O will represent the total yield of the trade tax which will be used to pay an income subsidy in A. Compare the point C_2 with C_3. The rate of trade tax in A will be $\dfrac{E_2O}{OD_2}$ instead of $\dfrac{E_3O}{OD_3}$. Now it is easy to show that $\dfrac{E_2O}{OD_2}$ is $> \dfrac{E_3O}{OD_3}$: in the first place, OD_2 is $<$ OD_3; and in the second place E_2O is $> E_3O$ (i) because C_2 is to the left of C_3 and (ii) because the slope of α_2 cannot be steeper than the slope of α_3 without B-exportables being an inferior good in A's consumption (see page 15 above). It follows that C_2 represents a trade point with a higher rate of trade tax in A than in the case of C_3. At C_1 the rate of trade tax $\left(\dfrac{E_1O}{OD_1}\right)$ will approach infinity, and at C_4 the rate of trade tax $\dfrac{E_4O}{OD_4}$ will be zero. Thus as we move from C_1 to C_4 we move along a line of decreasing rates of trade tax in A.

As C moves to the right of C_4 we move along a line of increasing trade subsidies in A. At C_5 the rate of trade subsidy is $\dfrac{E_5O}{OD_5}$ and at C_6 the rate of trade subsidy is $\dfrac{E_6O}{OD_6}$. It can be shown that $\dfrac{E_6O}{OD_6}$ is $> \dfrac{E_5O}{OD_5}$.

Now $\dfrac{E_6O}{OD_6} = 1 - \dfrac{E_6D_6}{OD_6}$ and $\dfrac{E_5O}{OD_5} = 1 - \dfrac{E_5D_5}{OD_5}$. It is, therefore, required to prove that $\dfrac{E_6D_6}{OD_6} < \dfrac{E_5D_5}{OD_5}$. This is so because, in the first place, OD_6 is $> OD_5$, and, secondly, E_6D_6 cannot be $> E_5D_5$ since $C_6D_6 = C_5D_5$ and, in the absence of inferior goods, the slope of α_6 cannot be less steep than that of α_5.

As the line C_1C_6 is moved up and down the point C_4 will trace out A's offer curve and the points C_2, C_3, C_5, C_6 will trace out curves showing offer curves for A modified by trade taxes at rates of $\dfrac{E_2O}{OD_2}$ and $\dfrac{E_3O}{OD_3}$ and trade subsidies at rates of $\dfrac{E_5O}{OD_5}$ and $\dfrac{E_6O}{OD_6}$ respectively. All these curves will pass through the origin O. The curve traced out by C_2 will always lie between the Y-axis and A's offer curve, and to the left of the curve traced out by C_3; and so on.

We can therefore draw for A a modified offer curve which will represent the position if A's trade is subjected to a trade tax or subsidy of a given *ad valorem* rate. And we can do the same for B. A trade tax in B will cause the modified offer curve B to lie between B's ordinary offer curve and the X-axis, and a trade subsidy in B will cause B's modified offer curve to rise above B's ordinary offer curve.

We can, therefore, proceed to draw a modified A-offer curve determined by the given rate of trade tax or subsidy in A and a modified B-offer curve determined by the given rate of trade tax or subsidy in B. Their point of intersection will give the trade point. For example, in Figure XXXI O_a and O_b are the normal offer curves. But O_a' is O_a modified by a rate of trade subsidy in A of $\dfrac{OG}{OH}$ and O_b' is O_b modified by a rate of trade tax in B of $\dfrac{OE}{OF}$. Then Q' is the trade point; and drawing α and β tangential to the A- and B-trade-indifference curves at Q' we derive the points E and G. Then OG is the total revenue in A which is raised in income tax and used to pay trade subsidies, and OE is the total revenue in B raised in trade taxation and used to pay income subsidies.

5

THE EFFECT OF PROTECTION UPON DOMESTIC PRODUCTION*

The imposition of a trade tax by country B will have the effect of shifting B's offer curve downwards (from O_b to O_b' in Figure XXXI). If country A does not impose any tax or subsidy the new position of trade equilibrium would be at the point J at which B's tax-modified offer curve (O_b') cuts A's free trade offer curve (O_a). In the initial free trade position the market price in B of A-exportables in terms of B-exportables will be equal to the slope of the line OQ, which is, of course, equal to the slope of the B-trade-indifference curve which passes through Q; after the imposition of the trade tax by B the market price in B of A-exportables in terms of B-exportables will be given by the slope of the B-trade-indifference curve which passes through J.

Will the slope of the B-trade-indifference curve which passes through J be steeper or less steep than that of the B-trade-indifference curve which passes through Q? If it is steeper, then the effect of the protective policy in B will have been to raise the price in B of A-exportables in terms of B-exportables; it will have raised the price of the product of the protected industry in B and will thus encourage the production of A-exportables at the expense of B-exportables in B, the extent of the encouragement depending upon the speed with which costs

* This section merely illustrates a point which Professor L. A. Metzler has made in his article "Tariffs, the Terms of Trade, and the Distribution of National Income" in the *Journal of Political Economy*, February 1949.

increase in B (i.e. upon the curvature of B's production block). But is it possible that the B-trade-indifference curve slopes less steeply through J than through Q? In this case we should have the paradoxical result that the protection of the A-exportable industry in B would *lower* the price of A-exportables in B and would thus *discourage* the production in B of the products of the protected industry.

Figures XXXII and XXXIII are devised to show in what conditions this paradoxical result may occur. In Figure XXXII Q represents the initial free trade point. Let us consider first of all what happens if A's offer curve has an elasticity greater than unity* and is thus of the shape shown by O_a^1 in the Figure. Then B's tax-modified offer curve will cut O_a^1 at some point such as C, D, or E on O_a^1 between O and Q. Consider first of all the point C at which O_a^1 is cut by I_{tb}, the B-trade-indifference curve which passes through the free trade point Q. It is obvious from the curvature of I_{tb} that the slope of I_{tb} at C is greater than at Q, i.e. that in this case protection will have the normal effect of raising the domestic market price of the protected commodity.

A fortiori will this be so if the rate of trade tax is even heavier so that the new position of trade equilibrium is at some point, such as D, which is on a lower B-trade-indifference curve. For if the B-trade-indifference curve which passed through D had already at D a slope which was less steep than OQ, we would clearly have to pass below and not above Q as we moved North-East from D along a trade-indifference curve whose slope became less and less steep. In other words the B-trade-indifference curve passing through D would cut I_{tb}, the B-trade-indifference curve which passes through Q. Therefore the slope of the B-trade-indifference curve at D must in fact be steeper than at Q.

* See page 88 below.

But the result is not quite so certain if we consider a point such as E at which the degree of protection in B is sufficiently moderate to have moved B on to a higher trade-indifference curve. Clearly it would be possible to draw a B-trade-indifference curve which passed through E and whose slope at E was less steep than the slope of I_{tb} at Q and which, nevertheless, did not cut I_{tb}. But since the slope of I_{tb} itself is steeper at the point F directly above E than at Q, it follows that the slope of the B-trade-indifference curve passing through E, if it were less steep than the slope of I_{tb} at Q, would *a fortiori* be less steep than the slope of I_{tb} at F. In other words in these circumstances A-exportables would be an "inferior" commodity in B's consumption.

In common-sense terms the meaning of this is as follows. If A's offer curve has an elasticity greater than unity, the protection of A-exportables in B might lower the price of A-exportables in B if both of two conditions were simultaneously fulfilled: (i) the degree of protection in B were sufficiently moderate to cause some real increase in welfare in B and (ii) A-exportables were such an inferior product in B's consumption that when consumers in B became better off they bought such a much smaller amount of A-exportables that this decline in B's home demand for them outweighed the direct effect of the protective duty in raising their prices.

Let us next consider the possibility that A's offer curve has an elasticity less than unity (O_a^2 instead of O_a^1 in Figure XXXII). It is now possible that the protection of A-exportables in B will lower their market price in B even though A-exportables are not an inferior commodity in B's consumption. This can readily be seen from Figure XXXII. Suppose that B's tax-modified offer curve cuts O_a^2 at G. At H, the point on I_{tb} immediately above G, the slope of I_{tb} will be less than at Q. If the slope of the B-trade-indifference curve which passes through G is intermediate between that of I_{tb} at Q and that of I_{tb} at H, then the protective policy will have lowered the market price in B of the protected A-exportables (the slope at G is less than at Q) but A-exportables will not be inferior commodities in B's consumption (the slope at G is greater than at H).

The meaning of this result is as follows. Since A's demand for B's product is inelastic, the restriction of trade due to B's trade tax causes A's traders to offer a greater total amount of B's products in return for a smaller total quantity of A's products (G lies South-East of Q). This may so greatly turn the barter terms of trade in B's favour by lowering the price at which A will provide A-exportables to B that, even when the tax is added, the market price of A-exportables in B is lower than in the initial free trade position.

We may conclude, then, that the normal result of protection will be to raise the market price, and so to encourage the output, of the protected product. But the opposite effect may occur if the marginal propensity to purchase the imported product in the protecting country (i.e. its desire to spend on imports any addition to its real purchasing power) is sufficiently low and if the elasticity of demand for its products in the other country is sufficiently small. It can be shown that the critical point at which the imposition of the duty in B will cause no change in market price relationships in B is when the marginal propensity to import in B plus the elasticity of demand for imports in A is equal to one. When this sum is less than one the price of the protected product will fall in B; when this sum is greater than one the price of the protected product will rise in B.

This can be seen from Figure XXXIII. Suppose that an import duty in B so modifies B's offer curve (O_b) that it cuts A's offer curve (O_a) at G instead of at Q. Through G draw the price line α_1 with the same slope as the free trade price line α. Suppose that the B-trade-indifference curve I_{tb} which passes through G does in fact have a slope at G which is less steep than α, so that I_{tb} cuts α_1 in the way shown in Figure XXXIII.* In this case the line α_1 must be tangential to a B-trade-indifference curve at some point to the left of G such as F. Draw the lines DEF, RSG, QSET, and QGU. Now the elasticity of A's offer curve between Q and G is equal to $\dfrac{OT}{OU}$ or, by similar triangles, $\dfrac{RS}{RG}$ (see page 88 below). And the marginal propensity to import in B is $\dfrac{EF}{DF}$, because when purchasing power in B goes up by DF measured in terms of A-exportables and prices remain unchanged, B's trading point moves from Q to F and only EF out of DF is used by B to purchase more imports of A-exportables (see page 86 below). But $\dfrac{EF}{DF} = \dfrac{EF}{RG}$, so that the elasticity of demand for imports in A plus the marginal propensity to import in B $= \dfrac{RS + EF}{RG}$. But since EF is less than SG, $\dfrac{RS + EF}{RG}$ is less than one. In other words, if I_{tb} is less steeply sloped than α_1 at G, this critical sum is less than unity.

Similarly it could be shown that if I_{tb} were more steeply sloped than α_1 at G, F would lie to the right of G, and the sum of the elasticity of demand for imports in A and the marginal propensity to import in B would be greater than one.

---

* The curve I_{tb} while it may be less steep than α_1 at G must be steeper than β at G for the following reason. Let the price line β cut O_b at C. If the equilibrium at Q is stable, C must be to the right of G. (See page 91 below.) At C there will be a B-trade-indifference curve with the same slope as β. At the point immediately left of C, I_{tb} must, in the absence of inferior goods, have a slope steeper than β. *A fortiori* its slope is steeper than β at G.

6

THE OPTIMUM DUTY

From the discussion of Figure XXXII in the previous section it will have become clear that if B imposes a trade tax and A does not retaliate B can move on to a higher indifference curve, provided that the rate of duty is not unduly high. Thus in Figure XXXII at any point between C and Q on O_a^1 B will be on a higher indifference curve than I_{tb}. B reaches her highest possible indifference curve if she imposes such a rate of duty that B's tax-modified offer curve cuts A's free trade offer curve at the point at which the latter is tangential to a B-trade-indifference curve. Such a point is illustrated by the point J on O_a^1; clearly B cannot choose to trade on any other point on O_a^1 which would place B on a higher indifference curve. As we have already seen, the rate of duty in B required to make J an equilibrium trading point is measured by $\dfrac{LO}{KO}$. But $\dfrac{LO}{KO} = \dfrac{LO}{JN} =$ (by similar triangles) $\dfrac{OM}{MN} = \dfrac{I}{\dfrac{OM + MN}{OM} - I} = \dfrac{I}{\dfrac{ON}{OM} - I}$. But, as we shall see later (page 88), $\dfrac{ON}{OM}$ measures the numerical value of the elasticity of A's offer curve at the point J. Thus we reach the conclusion that the rate of trade duty which will raise B on to the highest possible indifference curve (in the absence of retaliation from A) is equal to $\dfrac{I}{\epsilon - I}$, where ϵ is the numerical value of the elasticity of A's offer curve.

7

TAXES AND SUBSIDIES ON IMPORTS AND EXPORTS

So far in sections (4), (5), and (6) we have spoken merely of *trade* taxes or subsidies and have not distinguished between taxes or subsidies levied on *imports* or *exports*. As has already been shown (page 59), it makes no *real* difference whether the taxes are levied on export or import trade, though it does make a considerable monetary difference. It will be remembered that we are assuming domestic monetary policies in A and B which stabilize the domestic factor-cost price and market price* of A-exportables in terms of A's currency and of B-exportables in terms of B's currency. We can now distinguish between an export and an import tax in the geometric representations which we are using in this section.

Let the point Q in Figure XXXIV represent the point of intersection of B's ordinary offer curve (there being no trade taxes or subsidies in B) with A's offer curve as modified by a trade tax at the rate of $\frac{DO}{OG}$. Let $\frac{CO}{OG}$ represent the rate of export tax in A. Then we can show that $\frac{DC}{CG}$ will represent the rate of import tax in A.

In order to purchase GQ of B's money and so of B's products, importers in A have to pay CG of A's money. The slope of ϵ, therefore, represents the rate of exchange. But when B's importers use this CG of A's money to purchase A's products they have to pay CO in export duty on the OG of A's products which they actually purchase. The slope of β, therefore, represents the market price relationship in B and the barter terms of trade.

---

* We are assuming no indirect taxation or subsidies in A on A-exportables, so that the factor-cost price of A-exportables equals the market price of A-exportables in A. And similarly for B.

77

But A's importers when they bring in B's products have to pay DC in import duty on top of the CG which they have paid in the foreign exchange market for the purchase of QG of B's money, so that $\dfrac{DC}{CG}$ represents the *ad valorem* rate of import duty in A.

We have, then, $\dfrac{DO}{OG}$ equals the rate of trade tax (or t), $\dfrac{DC}{CG}$ the rate of import tax (or i), and $\dfrac{CO}{OG}$ the rate of export tax (or e). Now

$$t = \frac{DO}{OG} = \frac{DC}{OG} + \frac{CO}{OG} = \frac{DC}{CG} \cdot \frac{CG}{OG} + \frac{CO}{OG}$$
$$= \frac{DC}{CG} \left(1 + \frac{CO}{OG}\right) + \frac{CO}{OG}$$
$$= i\,(1 + e) + e = i + e + ie.$$

Thus, as we have defined the terms (and they are the natural definitions), the rate of trade taxation is equal to the rate of import tax plus the rate of export tax plus the product of the last two rates. This formula can be extended to cover the case of subsidies merely by treating subsidies as taxes with a negative sign.

In Figure XXXV we extend this analysis of the distinction between taxes on imports and exports to the case in which there are import and export taxes in both countries. Let Q represent the point of intersection of the A-offer curve modified by trade taxation at the rate $\dfrac{DO}{OG}$ and of a B-offer curve modified by trade taxation at the rate $\dfrac{FO}{OH}$. It follows that if we draw the α-line and β-line through Q tangential to the A- and B-trade-indifference curves which pass through Q, these lines will pass through D and F respectively.

Let $\dfrac{CO}{OG}$ and $\dfrac{EO}{OH}$ represent the export tax rates in A and B respectively, so that $\dfrac{DC}{CG}$ and $\dfrac{EF}{EH}$ represent, as we have just shown, the import tax rates. Draw the perpendicular GQ through Q and extend to J, so that $JQ = OE$; and similarly make $QK = CO$. Then CEKJ is a parallelogram and CJ and EK have the same slope; this slope marked ϵ will represent the rate of exchange. This can be seen by the following analysis.

Importers in A pay CG of A's money to purchase JG of B's money; but when they import the goods into A they have to pay an import duty of DC on top of the purchase price (CG) of the foreign exchange; and they have also to pay over QJ ($= OE$) of B's money to B's government in export duty on the QG ($= HO$) of goods purchased in B for export to A. Thus A's importers do pay in all DG in return for QG, i.e. at a price relationship α. Similarly importers in B pay HE ($= JG$) of their money for HK ($= CG$) of A's money; but when they import A's products they pay in addition EF of their own money in import duties to their own government and give up QK ($= CO$) of A's money to A's government in export duty on the HQ ($= OG$) of A's products which they do actually import.

CHAPTER VII

A Balance-of-Trade Deficit and the Rate of Exchange in Conditions of Free Trade

WE shall now turn from a consideration of Commercial Policy and shall assume once more that there is a free trade policy in both countries, A and B. But we no longer assume that the balance of trade of each country is zero. Our purpose in this section will be (*a*) to show how a balance-of-trade deficit or surplus can be represented on our geometric diagrams and (*b*) to consider the relationship, in a free trade world, between the size of the balance-of-trade deficit or surplus and the rate of exchange and barter terms of trade.

In considering the rate of exchange we shall make the same assumptions about internal monetary policies as we have previously made. In country A the monetary and fiscal authorities take steps to inflate the general level of domestic expenditure of money on goods and services whenever the price of A-exportables in terms of A's currency falls, and to deflate domestic expenditure in A whenever the price of A-exportables rises in terms of A's currency. Thus the demand price for A-exportables is fixed in terms of A's currency. Behind this fixed point, a free competitive market for A-exportables and B-exportables in A results in a price for B-exportables in terms of A's currency which will just clear the market in A for both commodities; and a free competitive market for labour causes the money wage-rate in A to rise (or to fall) when the demand for labour exceeds (or falls short of) the supply, so that full employment is maintained.

A similar monetary policy is adopted in B. The price of B-exportables in terms of B's currency is maintained constant by a suitable reflationary or disinflationary policy of domestic expenditure in B; and the price of A-exportables and of B's labour in terms of B's currency then adjust themselves to this fixed price of B-exportables so that the markets for both commodities and for labour in B are just cleared.

In our present model the rate of exchange between A's currency and B's currency will move in exactly the same way as the net barter terms of trade between A's products and B's products. The factor-cost price of A-exportables is fixed in terms of A's currency and the factor-cost price of B-exportables is fixed in terms of B's currency. In the absence of export duties and subsidies, which is part of our present free trade assumption, the net barter terms of trade are measured by the ratio between the factor-cost price of A's exports and the factor-cost price of B's exports, when these two prices have been reduced to a common unit by means of the rate of exchange between the two currencies. In other words $\frac{ep_a}{p_b}$ becomes the net barter terms of trade, where p_a is the factor-cost price of a unit of A's exports in terms of A's currency, e is the rate of foreign exchange (i.e. the number of units of B's money which can be obtained for a unit of A's), and p_b is the factor-cost price of a unit of B's exports in terms of B's currency. Our monetary assumption is that p_a and p_b are both constant, so that the net barter terms of trade vary directly with the rate of exchange e. If we choose units of currency so that the price of A-exportables is fixed at one in terms of A's currency and the price of B-exportables is fixed at one in terms of B's currency, then the net barter terms of trade are equal to the rate of foreign exchange.

We can now proceed to show how a balance-of-trade deficit or surplus can be shown on our geometric diagrams. Since we are assuming free trade, any point of equilibrium within A and B must result in the same market price relationship between A-exportables and B-exportables in the two markets. What in previous diagrams we have drawn as the α-price line and the β-price line must have the same slope. In other words the trading point Q must lie on the contract-curve, which is the locus of the points at which an A-trade-indifference curve is tangential to a B-trade-indifference curve.

In Figure XXXVI we take a point Q on the contract curve K-K′, and draw the common price line αβ through Q tangential to the A- and the B-trade-indifference curves at Q. Let this line cut the Y-axis at E and the X-axis at D. It is clear from what has just been said that the slope of the price line αβ which measures the rate at which A-exportables and B-exportables will exchange for each other in A and in B must also measure the net barter terms of trade between A and B and also the rate of exchange between A's and B's currencies.

The position in Figure XXXVI can be shown to represent a position in which, in conditions of free trade, country A has a balance-of-trade deficit of DO measured in terms of A's currency or A-exportables or of EO measured in terms of B's currency or B-exportables. The demonstration is as follows.

CD measures in units of A's currency the net national income earned from producing A-exportables and B-exportables in A; but CO must measure the level of domestic expenditure in A, since otherwise consumers would not be able to move up the price line α_1 from C to their consumption point.* DO therefore measures the balance-of-trade deficit in A; and in order to prevent

---

* It might be better to speak of "final buyers" and their "final-buying point" rather than of "consumers" and their "consumption point" because some of the uses of A- and B-exportables in A which are stimulated by the inflation of domestic expenditure in A may be uses for capital investment and not for current consumption in A.

this net inflow of goods on to A's market from causing a deflation in A, the authorities in A have to inflate domestic expenditure in A until it is larger than A's national income by DO. Similarly in B, the net national income in terms of B-exportables is EF, but domestic expenditure has to be deflated down to OF, because there is a net export surplus of OE which, by drawing goods from B's domestic market, would otherwise cause an inflationary movement in B. Since the slope of $\alpha\beta$ represents the rate of exchange between A's currency and B's currency, A's balance-of-trade deficit of DO, when converted into B's currency, is equal to B's balance-of-trade surplus of EO.

A's balance-of-trade deficit may be covered in many different ways. It might be covered by a direct payment from B's government to A's government of Marshall Aid or of reparations; and such a direct grant might be fixed at EO in terms of B's currency or at DO in terms of A's currency. Or the deficit may be covered by a movement of long-term capital, or short-term capital, or of monetary reserves. Now the analysis which we are developing in this section may be used to find answers to two different types of question.

(i) Given the rate of exchange ($\alpha\beta$) what will be the deficit or surplus on a country's balance of trade, which will have to be financed in one way or another—if necessary by a flow of monetary reserves?

(ii) Given a certain transfer element in the balance of payments (e.g. Marshall Aid, reparations, a normal flow of long-term capital) what is the rate of exchange which will adjust the balance of trade so that it fits in with these transfer items and no accommodating movement of monetary reserves is needed?

When we are dealing with questions of the second type it makes a great difference whether the transfer items are fixed in terms of A's currency or of B's currency, since an alteration in the rate of exchange which is necessary in order to generate the balance-of-trade deficit or surplus needed to fit in with the transfer items will itself affect those transfer items differently according as they are themselves fixed in the one currency or the other.

Consider any point G on the line QD in Figure XXXVI. This could be taken to represent the fact that there were transfers in the balance of payments between A and B of OJ from B to A fixed in terms of B's currency and of OH from A to B fixed in terms of A's currency.* At the rate of exchange $\alpha\beta$ this will be equivalent to a net transfer from B to A of DO measured in A's currency or EO measured in B's currency. But if the exchange rate were altered to the slope of γ this would represent a net transfer in the opposite direction from A to B of OL measured in A's money or of OM measured in B's currency.

Now in our free trade world internal equilibrium in A and in B is to be obtained only when the trading point Q is on the contract curve K-K'; and the size of any deficit or surplus in the balance of trade is measured by the point at which the price line or exchange-rate line from the relevant point on the contract curve cuts the X-axis and the Y-axis. In order, therefore, to examine the relationship between balance-of-trade deficits and surpluses and the rate of exchange, we must examine the way in which the slope of the price line changes as we move up and down the contract curve. Our next task will be to establish two propositions in this respect:—

* We can generalize this by saying that from any point G in any of the four quadrants we draw lines perpendicular to the X-axis and the Y-axis. The distance between O and the point on the X-axis directly under or above G represents a transfer fixed in A's currency; and the transfer is from A to B if the point is to the right of O and from B to A if it is to the left of O. The distance between O and the point on the Y-axis level with G represents a transfer fixed in B's currency; and the transfer is from B to A if the point is above O and from A to B if the point is below O.

(i) First, if the sum of the marginal propensities to import in the two countries is less than unity, the slope of the price line $\alpha\beta$ (Figure XXXVI) will become steeper and steeper as we move from South-East to North-West up the contract curve.

(ii) Second, if the sum of the price elasticities of what we shall call the net demand for net imports in the two countries is greater than unity, then as we move up the contract curve from South-East to North-West the price line $\alpha\beta$ will cut the appropriately adjusted X-axis at a higher point and the appropriately adjusted Y-axis at a point further to the left.

Figure XXXVII is constructed to demonstrate the truth of the first of these two propositions. Through the point Q on the contract curve K-K′ draw the price line α which is tangential to the A- and the B-trade-indifference curve which passes through Q. Draw another price line, α', parallel to α and above α by an amount equal to QE. The shift from α to α' would represent a state of affairs in which the deficit on A's balance of trade and the surplus on B's balance of trade had increased by HJ (or QE) from OH to OJ in terms of B's currency, without any change in the rate of exchange between A's currency and B's currency. In order to preserve internal balance in A the authorities in A would have to inflate domestic expenditure in A by an amount equal to EQ (measured in units of B's currency). Similarly the authorities in B would have to deflate domestic expenditure in B by an amount equal to HJ.

When this policy of inflating domestic expenditure in A by HJ had been carried out, the corner of A's production block would have moved up from Q to some point on the new price line α'. It will, of course, move to the point at which the price line α is tangential to the highest A-trade-indifference curve. Suppose this point to be F. Then this represents a state of affairs in which the marginal propensity to import in country A is equal to $\dfrac{CQ}{QE}$. The increase in domestic expenditure in A is QE and the increase in the amount of B-exportables imported into A is CQ; and since the price of B-exportables is fixed in terms of B's currency, CQ also represents the increase in expenditure (in terms of B's currency) on imports into A. If we define the marginal propensity to import as the ratio between the increase in expenditure on imports and the increase in the domestic expenditure (*not* the increase in the national income) which causes it, then $\dfrac{CQ}{QE}$ measures the marginal propensity to import in A.

And similarly for B. Domestic expenditure in B falls by QE. As a result of this the corner of B's production block will move from Q to a point G at which a B-trade-indifference curve is tangential to the new price line α'. GD now measures the decrease in B's imports from A, and at the net barter terms of trade and exchange rate α' this has a value ED in terms of B's currency. Thus $\dfrac{ED}{QE}$ measures the marginal propensity to import in B.

Now the sum of the marginal propensities to import in the two countries is $\dfrac{CQ + ED}{QE}$, and if this is less than one, CQ + ED is less than QE. In other words, in this case D will lie above C, so that G will lie above and to the right of F. But from inspection of Figure XXXVII it can be intuitively seen that if there is a B-trade-indifference curve tangential to α' at G and an A-trade-indifference curve tangential to α' at F, then intermediate between F and G on the line α' there will be a point at which B- and A-trade-indifference curves are tangential, and that the slope of this tangent (β) will be steeper than α'. In other words we have proved our first proposition to the effect that, as we move from the South-East to the North-West up the contract curve K-K′ the slopes of the tangents to the trade-indifference curves will become steeper (β is steeper than α) if the sum of the marginal propensities to import is less than one.

Our second proposition on page 85 concerns the price elasticities of demand in the two countries; and Figure XXXVIII has been constructed in order to show how these elasticities may be measured geometrically. As we have already stated, the relevant price elasticity for each country is what we shall call the elasticity of that country's net demand for net imports. We must now explain what is meant by this.

Let us suppose (Figure XXXVIII) that an amount fixed at OH in terms of A's currency and so, on our monetary assumptions, in terms of A-exportables is being paid in an autonomous transfer from A to B (e.g. reparations, Marshall Aid, etc.), and that an amount fixed at OJ in B's currency or B-exportables is similarly being transferred from B to A. Then in any position of equilibrium A will always be receiving imports of OJ or GH without having to export anything to purchase them and B will always be importing OH or JG without having to export anything in return. The amount of trade GH for JG is, as it were, predetermined and fixed regardless of any changes in the terms of trade or other factors which normally determine the volume of trade. What we are now interested in is the additional amounts of trade which traders in each country will wish to conduct at various prices.

This can be shown in the following way. Take the point G instead of the point O in Figure XXXVIII as the origin and let successive price lines such as α and β be drawn from this origin G. Suppose that S and R are points at which A-trade-indifference curves are tangential to α and β respectively. Then the locus of these points S and R is A's offer curve for trade additional to the fixed amount represented by the point G. It is the elasticity of this offer curve which we call the elasticity of A's net demand for net imports (i.e. the additional exports above JG which she will give for additional imports above HG).

Let us consider the measurement of the elasticity of this curve between the points S and R. Join S and R and extend the line to cut JG extended at D. Drop perpendiculars SF and RC on to JG extended, and SN and RP on to HG extended. Let β cut NS at T. Draw a vertical line through T to cut PR at V and GC at E. Now the proportional increase in the quantity of net imports purchased by A between S and R is $\frac{PN}{NG} = \frac{VT}{NG} =$, by similar triangles, $\frac{VR}{NT} = \frac{EC}{GE}$. The proportional increase in price between R and S is $\frac{TS}{NT} \left(= \frac{EF}{GE} \right)$, since for an import of B-exportables of NG A would have to give NT of A-exportables at the price β and NT + TS at the price α. The proportional change in quantity divided by the proportional change in price is, therefore, $\frac{EC}{GE} \div \frac{EF}{GE}$ or $\frac{EC}{EF}$. But $\frac{EC}{EF} = \frac{TU}{TS} =$, by similar triangles, $\frac{GC}{GD}$. Thus the ratio $\frac{GC}{GD}$ measures the elasticity of the offer curve O_a between the points R and S. If now we let R and S approach one another so that we are measuring the "point" elasticity and not the "arc" elasticity, the line DS will become the tangent to the offer curve at the relevant point. For example, if we consider the point M on

B's offer curve O_b, $\dfrac{GK}{GL}$ measures the elasticity of O_b at the point M.*

From these formulae it is clear that the price elasticity of net demand for net imports in A is greater than one so long as D lies to the left of C, but becomes less than one as D moves to the right of C. Similarly, the price elasticity of net demand for net imports in B becomes less than one as L moves above K.

Let us now confine our attention to the elasticities of the two offer curves at their point of intersection (i.e. at Q in Figure XXXVIII). In Figure XXXIX we show a case where both elasticities are less than one and where D has moved so far to the right of C and L has moved so far above K that LQD forms a straight line. In this case the sum of the two elasticities is equal to unity. This can be shown as follows. The sum of the two elasticities is $\dfrac{GC}{GD} + \dfrac{GK}{GL}$. But $\dfrac{GK}{GL} = \dfrac{CQ}{GL}$ and since LQD is a straight line we have by similar triangles $\dfrac{CQ}{GL} = \dfrac{CD}{GD}$. Therefore $\dfrac{GC}{GD} + \dfrac{GK}{GL} = \dfrac{GC}{GD} + \dfrac{CD}{GD} = 1$.

Suppose now that D in Figure XXXIX moves a little nearer C, so that the sum of the two elasticities is now greater than unity. In other words the line QD pivots round on Q so that D approaches C, the line LQ remaining unchanged. Remembering that QD is tangential to O_a at Q and QL tangential to O_b at Q, we can see that, in this case in which the sum of the elasticities is greater than unity, as we move along O_a from the origin G towards Q the curve O_a will cut the curve O_b at the point Q from inside the arc of the

* This is the formula given by Professor Lerner in his article on "The Diagrammatical Representation of Elasticity of Demand" in *The Review of Economic Studies* for October 1933. The form of the proof which I have given was suggested to me by Mr. Ozga of the London School of Economics.

curve O_b. Conversely, if either of the two elasticities of net demand became a little smaller (D moved to the right or L moved upwards in Figure XXXIX), LQ would have a steeper downward slope than QD. In this case, in which the sum of the elasticities of net demand would be less than unity, it is clear that as one moved along O_a from the origin G towards the point of intersection Q, O_a would cut O_b at Q from outside the arc of the curve O_b.*

In passing it may be interesting to observe that if the sum of the marginal propensities to import is equal to, or greater than, unity then the sum of the elasticities of net demand for net imports must be greater than unity. This is shown geometrically in Figure XL. We start with the relevant origin for the offer curves at G and with an equilibrium trading point on the contract curve at D, such that the price line α which is tangential to the trade-indifference curves at this point passes through G. If the sum of the marginal propensities to import were equal to one, then we could take another point on the contract curve at C, and the line $α_1$ which was drawn through C parallel to α would also be tangential to the two trade-indifference curves which pass through C. It is clear from the figure that in this case, if one swings the price line α round on a pivot at G until it passes through C (i.e. until it takes up the position of β in the figure), there will be a B-trade-indifference curve tangential to β to the right of C as at N and an A-trade-indifference curve tangential to β to the left of C as at M. The A-offer curve will pass through M and D and the B-offer curve through N and D; and the two offer curves will cut at D in the way which shows that the sum of the two price elasticities is greater than one.†

* Q would then correspond to the point D in Figure XXVII.

† Suppose $x = \phi\,(E, p)$ to.represent any demand function, where $x =$ the quantity of the commodity which is demanded, E the total money expenditure

In passing it is important to remember the familiar proposition that the position of equilibrium in the foreign trade market will be stable if the sum of the two price elasticities of net demand for net imports is greater than one. This can also be seen from Figure XL. Suppose we start at the trade-equilibrium point D with a price line α. Suppose for some reason that there is a small accidental disturbance of this price line, so that it moves to β. At this point the demand in B for A's exports is OF but the supply of exports by A is only OE; the price of A's exports will be driven up again from β towards α. The same analysis can, of course, be done in terms of B's exports. The demand for B's exports in A is EM and the supply from B is FN. The supply exceeds the demand in the foreign market and the price of B's exports will fall from β towards α. Thus when the

available to be spent on this or on the alternative commodities, and $p =$ the price of this commodity. Differentiating we have $\dfrac{p}{x} \cdot \dfrac{dx}{dp} = \dfrac{p}{x} \cdot \dfrac{\delta x}{\delta E} \cdot \dfrac{dE}{dp} + \dfrac{p}{x} \cdot \dfrac{\delta x}{\delta p}$.

The last term $\dfrac{p}{x} \cdot \dfrac{\delta x}{\delta p}$ measures the ordinary price elasticity of demand, price varying but total money expenditure available remaining constant. But suppose we vary the total money expenditure available for consumption in such a way that the consumer could have bought the same quantities of all commodities after the price change which in fact he bought before the price change, i.e. we assume $dE = xdp$. Then we have $\dfrac{p}{x} \cdot \dfrac{dx}{dp} = p\dfrac{\delta x}{\delta E} + \dfrac{p}{x} \cdot \dfrac{\delta x}{\delta p}$. We may call the resulting price elasticity of demand $\left(\dfrac{p}{x} \cdot \dfrac{dx}{dp}\right)$ the expenditure-compensated price elasticity of demand; and it measures the extent to which the consumer will substitute the one commodity for others when its relative price changes, abstracting from the fact that he buys more (or less) because he has a greater (or smaller) total real purchasing power when the price of the particular produce goes down (or up). The term $p\dfrac{dx}{\delta E}$ measures the marginal propensity to spend on the commodity in question, when its price remains unchanged but the total available purchasing power varies. Write $-\varepsilon$ for the ordinary price elasticity of demand, $-\varepsilon'$ for the expenditure-compensated price elasticity of demand, and π for the marginal propensity to import, then $\varepsilon = \pi + \varepsilon'$. It is clear then that the price elasticity of demand is equal to the marginal propensity to import plus a pure substitution factor. If there is any substitution factor at all it follows that the sum of the marginal propensities to import is less than the sum of the price elasticities of demand.

offer curves cut in the way shown in Figure XL (i.e. when the sum of the two price elasticities is greater than one), the point of intersection of the two offer curves will provide, not only a point of equilibrium, but also a point of stable equilibrium.

We can now put together the two propositions enunciated on page 85 and see what they imply. This is done in Figure XLI. Compare the two points C and D on the contract curve K-K'. Draw the price line α through C and the price line β'' through D, in each case tangential to the trade-indifference curves which pass through C and D. Now we know that if the sum of the marginal propensities to import is less than one, the slope of β'' will be steeper than that of α. It will therefore cut α at some point O''. Take any point O' on the line α to the right of O'', and draw the price line O'D or β'. It is clear from the figure that the line β' will be tangential to an A-trade-indifference curve at a point M above D and to a B-trade-indifference curve at a point N below D. The A-offer curve for the origin O' will, therefore, run from C to M and the B-offer curve for the origin O' will run from N to C. The sum of the elasticities of net demand for net imports at C will be greater than unity, if we take the origin of the offer curves from O'.

If, however, we take the origin of the offer curves at O'', the point of intersection of the α-line and β''-line, then the point D as well as the point C is on both offer curves. From the origin O'', therefore, the offer curves coincide in the region DC and the sum of the elasticities of net demand for net imports is equal to unity.

If we take a point O''' on α to the left of O'', and draw the price line O'''D or β''', then we could show that the point N would now lie on β''' to the right of D and the point M on β''' to the left of D, and the sum of the elasticities of net demand for net imports would be less than unity.

If, however, we stick to origins for the relevant offer curves which are on the α-line to the right of O'',* we can show that there are the two following normal relationships between the balance-of-trade deficit and the rate of exchange or barter terms of trade.

(i) An appreciation in A's exchange rate or improvement in A's barter terms of trade will worsen A's balance of payments; and

(ii) if there is an increase in autonomous transfers from B to A, A's exchange rate will have to be appreciated, i.e. B's barter terms of trade worsened, in order to avoid a balance-of-payments deficit for B.

Proposition (i) can be shown as follows. Suppose we are in equilibrium at C in Figure XLI with the price line α and with a balance-of-trade deficit for A made up of a transfer of OE from A to B and of EO' from B to A. Suppose then that A's exchange rate is appreciated to the slope of β''. Equilibrium will be found only at the point D at which the new price line β'' is tangential to the trade-indifference curves on the contract curve K-K'. But though β'' is steeper than α, it will lie above O' because O' is to the right of O''. In this sense, then, the appreciation of A's exchange rate will necessarily have worsened A's *balance of payments*. Whereas before the exchange-rate change, a transfer of OE from A to B and of EO' from B to A was needed to balance the balance of payments, now with a transfer of OE from A to B there must be combined a transfer of EH from B to A to balance the balance of payments.

But while in the conditions postulated it follows that

* This means that we are assuming that any autonomous transfer fixed in A's currency is either from A to B or else, if it is from B to A, must be less than OF in amount. There must also, of course, with any transfer fixed in terms of A's currency within these limits be associated that transfer fixed in B's currency which is necessary to bring the offer-curve origin on to the line α.

A's *balance of payments* will be worsened by an appreciation of A's currency it does not follow that A's *balance of trade* will be worsened. It *is* worsened in the particular example shown in Figure XLI. Before the appreciation of A's exchange rate A's balance-of-trade deficit was PO when measured in A's currency and SO when measured in B's currency; after the appreciation of A's currency it is QO and RO measured in these two currencies respectively. It is unambiguously greater.

But this is only because we have put the point O″ of intersection between the α-line and the β″-line in the quadrant X′OY′. It might lie in the quadrant X′OY. In this case it can be seen that while R would lie above S, Q would lie to the right of P. In the original position there is an excess of imports into A; when the exchange rate appreciates there is some increase in this deficit measured in B's currency; but the appreciation of A's currency is such as to make the balance-of-trade deficit somewhat smaller when valued in terms of A's currency.

There is an even more extreme possibility. The point O″ might lie in the quadrant XOY; this is quite compatible with O′ lying to the right of O″ which is our only present restriction. In this case it can be seen that R would lie below S as well as Q lying to the right of P. In this case a very large appreciation of A's exchange rate is required as the trading point moves from the point C to the point D along the contract curve. The shift in the trading point is very small compared with the change in the exchange rate; A does import somewhat more but not much more, and export somewhat less but not much less, in quantity; but A's products and currency are worth so much more per unit of B's products and currency that, whether measured in the one or the other, the excess of A's imports over her exports falls in value. Indeed it is even possible that A's balance-of-trade deficit turns into a balance-of-trade surplus if O″ is so near to O′ that DO″ extended passes to the South-East of O, so that Q is to the right of O and R is below O.

But all this is compatible with a worsening of A's balance of payments. H is still above O′, because O″ is to the left of O′. With the autonomous transfer of OE paid in A's currency from A to B we need a larger transfer (EH instead of EO′) to be paid in B's currency from B to A if we are to avoid a balance-of-payments deficit. What has happened is that the appreciation of A's currency has so increased the value (in terms of B's currency) of A's fixed transfer to B and so decreased the value (in terms of A's currency) of B's fixed transfer to A, that a balance-of-payments deficit has appeared for A equal to O′H in terms of B's currency, even though A's balance-of-trade deficit might, in the extreme case, even have turned into a surplus.

We can now turn to the second proposition on page 85. This can be easily demonstrated. We start in full equilibrium at the trading point C, the rate of exchange α, and the origin O′, i.e. with an autonomous transfer of OE from A to B plus an autonomous transfer of EO′ from B to A. We increase EO′ to EH. Our problem is to find the slope of the new price line β″ through H and to prove that it is steeper than α. We now bring a price line β″ through H round from a vertical position until it cuts the contract curve at a point at which β″ is tangential to the A- and B-trade-indifference curves at that point. This point cannot be to the South-East of C. Otherwise β″ would cut α to the right of O′, and we are assuming that O′ is to the right of O″, since we are assuming that the sum of the elasticities of net demand for net imports is greater than one. Therefore the point D is to the North-East of C. But if the sum of the marginal propensities to import is less than one, as we move North-East along K-K′ the slopes of the relevant price lines will become steeper and steeper. Therefore β'' is steeper than α, and A's exchange rate must be appreciated to preserve external balance when an additional transfer of O'H is made from B to A.

It is clear, then, that in our present model with free trade and with internal monetary policies which preserve full employment with a constant price in terms of each country's currency for its own exportable product, there is a unique relationship between the exchange rate or the barter terms of trade and the balance-of-trade surplus or deficit as measured in each currency. Turning back to Figure XXXVI, we can do either of two things. First, if we are given the exchange rate $\alpha\beta$ we can tell what the balance-of-trade position will be. In this case we move up the contract curve from South-East to North-West at each point reaching a position where a steeper and steeper price line is required for equilibrium. We stop at the point at which this slope is equal to that of the given rate of exchange. We then draw the line $\alpha\beta$ through this point Q and the balance-of-trade deficit of A is DO in terms of A's currency and EO in terms of B's currency.

Secondly, we can start from a given balance-of-payments position and find what exchange rate is necessary to give external equilibrium. For example, we can start from the position G in Figure XXXVI which represents a fixed transfer of OH of A's currency from A to B and of OJ of B's currency from B to A. Through G we turn a price line through successive slopes γ, $\alpha\beta$, etc. When we reach the position at which this price line cuts the contract curve at a slope which is the same as that of the tangents to the two trade-indifference curves at that point, we have found the equilibrium exchange rate.

CHAPTER VIII

The General Case

WE can now combine the various points which we have examined separately. In Figure XLII we show a position in which there is equilibrium with import and export taxes in both countries and with a balance-of-trade deficit for A and surplus for B.

Consider the trading point Q in Figure XLII. Through Q draw the price lines α and β tangential to the A- and the B-trade-indifference curves which pass through Q. Similarly draw α_1 and β_1 tangential to the A- and the B-consumption-indifference curves and production blocks at C and K respectively. Next draw QT equal to the total revenue raised in A on export taxes and QU equal to the total revenue raised in B in export taxes and complete the rectangle UQTQ'. Suppose that A's total deficit equals GO. Draw the line ϵ joining G and Q'. Mark off FG equal to QT and PN equal to UQ. Then the slope of ϵ will represent the rate of exchange between A's money and B's money, and EF and NM will represent the import taxes in A and B respectively, which must be imposed in order to give an equilibrium at Q with a balance-of-trade deficit for A of GO and with export taxes of QT and QU in A and B respectively.

We can first of all show that both countries will be in internal equilibrium in these conditions. In order that C should represent the consumption point in A, A's consumers must have DO to spend, and they then move up A's market price line α_1 to C. Now DE represents the national income at factor cost in A; EF and FG represent the revenue from import and export taxes, so that EG equals the income subsidies paid by A's government out of the revenue from indirect taxes; and GO represents the total amount of transfers from abroad (by way of reparations, foreign borrowing, etc.) which can also supplement the purchasing power of A's final buyers. Thus DO does in fact represent the total purchasing power in A measured in A's currency or in units of A-exportables.

Similarly in B, LM measures the net national income at factor cost; MN plus NP is the subsidy to income paid in B out of the revenue from import and export taxes; and PO measures B's balance-of-trade surplus (i.e. GO converted at the exchange rate ϵ), which represents a transfer of purchasing power away from B and which must, therefore, be deducted from B's internal purchasing power. Thus the internal purchasing power in B = LM + MN + NP − PO = LO.

We can also see that the position shown in Figure XLII represents a position of equilibrium in the foreign trade markets. Consumers in A consume QH of imported B-exportables, and at the market price α they pay EH for these imports. This amount EH is made up in the following way. Importers in A at the foreign exchange rate ϵ pay GJ for an amount of B's foreign money equal to Q'J, or (since FG = QT = HJ) an amount FH of A's money for an amount UH of B's money. With this UH they buy QH of B-exportables in B and pay UQ to B's government in export tax. The traders when they bring the QH of B's products into A have to add EF to the price to cover the import taxes which A's government levies. Thus EH does represent the final price which the traders will demand from consumers in A for the import of QH of B's products.

Similarly, at the price line β consumers in B give up RM of B's money for RQ of A's products. This price is made up as follows. Traders in B give up SP of their money at the foreign exchange rate ϵ to obtain SQ' or

OJ of A's money. This gives equilibrium in the foreign exchange market because, as we saw in the previous paragraph, A's traders are giving up GJ of A's money for Q'J or SO of B's money. A's traders are therefore offering GO of A's money in excess of what B's traders are buying, and are buying PO of B's money in excess of what B's traders are offering. But this (GO in A's money or PO in B's money) represents the balance-of-trade deficit which we are assuming to be financed by some other transfer. B's traders, then, having acquired SQ' of A's money for SP of their own, i.e. RT of A's money for RN of B's money, use this RT of A's money to purchase RQ of A's products and to pay QT in export tax to A's government. When the RQ of A's products are imported into B an import tax of NM is levied, so that the final price paid for the imports of RQ into B is RM, which does in fact correspond to the market price line β.

It may be of interest at this point to show certain simple relationships between the slopes of the price lines α, β, and ϵ. Consider first of all the market price line β. This must be equal to the total market expenditure in B on imports divided by the volume of imports. Thus $\beta = \dfrac{RM}{RQ} = \dfrac{SP + NM}{RQ}$. Write Q_a for total volume of A's exports, E_a for the total value in A's currency of export taxes in A, and I_b for the total value of import taxes in B in terms of B's currency. Then, as can be seen from Figure XLII, $SP = \epsilon\,(Q_a + E_a)$, $NM = I_b$, and $RQ = Q_a$, so that $\beta = \epsilon\left(1 + \dfrac{E_a}{Q_a} + \dfrac{1}{\epsilon}\cdot\dfrac{I_b}{Q_a}\right)$. Let us write e_a for the *ad valorem* rate of export taxes in A and i_b for the *ad valorem* rate of import taxes in B. Then $e_a = \dfrac{E_a}{Q_a}$; but $i_b = \dfrac{I_b}{\epsilon(Q_a + E_a)}$ which equals $\dfrac{1}{\epsilon}\cdot\dfrac{I_b}{Q_a}\cdot\dfrac{1}{1 + e_a}$, so that $\dfrac{1}{\epsilon} \cdot \dfrac{I_b}{Q_a} = i_b (1 + e_a)$. It follows that $\beta = \epsilon (1 + e_a + i_b + e_a i_b)$.

It can similarly be shown that $\alpha = \epsilon \left(\dfrac{1}{1 + e_b + i_a + e_b i_a} \right)$, where $e_b = \dfrac{E_b}{Q_b}$ the *ad valorem* rate of export taxes in B and $i_a = \dfrac{I_a}{\frac{1}{\epsilon}(Q_b + E_b)}$, the *ad valorem* rate of import taxes in A.

It can also be seen in Figure XLII that GO, which measures A's balance-of-trade deficit, $= GJ - OJ = \dfrac{1}{\epsilon}(Q_b + E_b) - (Q_a + E_a)$. This is equal to the value in terms of A's currency of the amount of B's currency bought for the purchase of B's exports and for the payment of export duty on these less the value in terms of A's currency of A's exports and the export duty payable on them. Similarly, B's balance-of-trade surplus $PO = SO - SP = Q_b + E_b - \epsilon(Q_a + E_a)$.

Finally, we may show the way in which the barter terms of trade can be represented on Figure XLII. The gross barter terms of trade present no difficulty at all; they are the ratio of total imports into A over total exports from A or $\dfrac{Q_b}{Q_a}$. They would be represented by the slope of the line (not drawn in Figure X LII) joining the consumption origin O and the production origin Q.

But the net barter terms of trade present rather more difficulty. They represent the net price in terms of A's currency obtained from foreigners for a unit of A's exports divided by the net price in terms of A's currency obtained by foreigners for a unit of B's exports. This is equal to $\dfrac{Q_a + E_a}{Q_a} \div \dfrac{\frac{1}{\epsilon}(Q_b + E_b)}{Q_b} = \dfrac{Q}{Q_a} \cdot \dfrac{\epsilon(Q_a + E_a)}{Q_b + E_b}$

$= \epsilon \, \dfrac{1 + e_a}{1 + e_b}$. We can derive this same result in a different manner. $\epsilon(Q_a + E_a)$ is the amount paid by B in B's currency for B's imports and $Q_b + E_b$ is the amount received by B in B's currency for her exports so that $\dfrac{\epsilon(Q_a + E_a)}{Q_b + E_b}$ is the proportion of B's exports which is required to finance her imports. Now Q_b is the total of B's exports so that $Q_b \cdot \dfrac{\epsilon(Q_a + E_a)}{Q_b + E_b}$ is the amount of B's exports required to finance her imports, so that $\dfrac{Q_b \cdot \dfrac{\epsilon(Q_a + E_a)}{(Q_b + E_b)}}{Q_a}$ is B's net barter terms of trade, which is the same result as that which we previously reached.

Figure XLIII shows how this expression $\dfrac{Q_b}{Q_a} \cdot \dfrac{\epsilon(Q_a + E_a)}{Q_b + E_b}$ may be represented geometrically. The points S, R, P, O, H, and Q in Figure XLIII are reproduced from Figure XLII. The gross barter terms of trade $\dfrac{Q_b}{Q_a}$ or $\dfrac{QH}{OH}$ is there represented by the slope of the line γ. For the representation of the net barter terms of trade, draw SQ and produce to cut the X-axis at W. Draw PW to cut QH at V. Draw V'H equal to VQ. Join OV' and the slope of this line γ' is the net barter terms of trade.

The proof is as follows. The slope of γ' is $\dfrac{V'H}{OH}$

$= \dfrac{VQ}{OH} = \dfrac{QH}{OH} \cdot \dfrac{VQ}{QH} =$, by similar triangles, $\dfrac{QH}{OH} \cdot \dfrac{SP}{SO}$

$= \dfrac{Q_b}{Q_a} \cdot \dfrac{\epsilon(Q_a + E_a)}{Q_b + E_b}$ which, we have just seen, measures the net barter terms of trade.

Figures XLII and XLIII do, therefore, show how to represent geometrically the general case. But there are various ways in which one can arrive at the general case. We will illustrate these ways in the form of three problems :—

(i) In Problem I we are given all the *ad valorem* rates of import and export duty in both countries, and we are given the rate of exchange between the currencies of the two countries. We have to find what will be the resulting deficit or surplus in the balance of trade which will be necessary to give full equilibrium in these conditions.

(ii) In Problem II we are given the rate of exchange and the balance-of-trade deficit, and we are also given all the *ad valorem* rates of import and export duties in the two countries, except the *ad valorem* rate of import duty in country A. This we have to find. In other words, our problem is to see what degree of import restriction is necessary in a given country to keep its deficit down to a certain given figure, when the exchange rate and all other elements of commercial policy are given.

(iii) In Problem III we are given all the *ad valorem* rates of import and export duty in both countries, and we are given the deficit in the balance of trade which can be financed in equilibrium. We have to find what is the rate of exchange which will be compatible with this equilibrium.

In order to solve the first two problems we shall have to introduce the idea of a map of trade-expenditure curves for each country. This is done in Figures XLIV, XLV, and XLVI.

An A-trade-expenditure curve of a given value is the locus of all points in the trade quadrant XOY at which the A-trade-indifference curves have a slope of that given value. Thus in Figure XLIV α_1 is parallel to α'_1, and both represent slopes of one in one. C and D are both points at which A-trade-indifference curves I_a and I'_a have similar slopes, and these points therefore lie on the A-trade-expenditure curve E_{a1} which shows the locus of all such points. If we assume that neither A-exportables nor B-exportables are inferior goods in A's consumption, then we can see that the A-trade-expenditure curve will have a negative slope throughout.

If we now move up the indifference curves I_a and I'_a in a north-easterly direction the slope will become steeper and steeper, until we reach points where the slope is two in one instead of one in one. Here we reach points on E_{a2}, which represents the locus of points at which the tangents to the A-trade-indifference curves have slopes of two in one. Because of the convexity of the A-trade-indifference curves, E_{a2} will clearly always lie North-East of E_{a1}.

It can similarly be seen from Figure XLIV that, if the B-trade-indifference curves are also convex and if there are no inferior goods in B's consumption, then the B-trade-expenditure curves will also always be negatively sloped and the higher-numbered B-trade-expenditure curve will always be to the South-West of a lower-numbered curve.

If we assume that the sum of the marginal propensities to import into the two countries is less than one, then we can set another important restriction upon the trade-expenditure-curve maps. This restriction can be stated as follows. At a point of intersection between an A- and a B-trade-expenditure curve, the A-trade-expenditure curve *must* have a gentler negative slope than the B-trade-expenditure curve if the B-curve is not lower-numbered than the A-curve, and this *may* also be the case if the B-curve is lower-numbered.

This result is illustrated in Figure XLV. Let us start with the position in section (2) of Figure XLV where we start in a position at C where the α-line and the β-line both have the same slope. Suppose now an amount of purchasing power FC is transferred from B to A. Then $\dfrac{DC}{FC}$ measures A's marginal propensity to import and $\dfrac{FE}{FC}$ measures B's marginal propensity to import. If the sum of these two is less than one, then D is below E, and G is to the left of H. It follows that E_{a_1}, which passes through G and C, is more gently sloped than E_{b_1}, which passes through H and C.

This result is even more clearly marked in section (1) of Figure XLV where at the point C the β-line is steeper than the α-line. Again FC of purchasing power is transferred from B to A and D lies below E. Now the only difference between this and the position in section (2) is that the β'-line has swivelled round on the point F until its slope is two in one instead of one in one. It is therefore closer to E, and E_{b_2} is therefore more steeply sloped in relation to E_{a_1} than was the case in section (2).

In section (3) of Figure XLV the lines β_1 and β_1' are as in section (2). It is now the α'-line which swivels round on the point F, thus bringing the point G nearer to D. If α' is sufficiently steeply sloped the point G will pass to the left of E_{b_1}, even though D remains below E. In this case, which is illustrated in section (3), E_{a_2} is more steeply sloped than E_{b_1} at their point of intersection.

Figure XLVI shows the general nature of the map of A- and B-trade-expenditure curves on the assumptions made above. We start with the contract curve K-K' which is the locus of the intersections of E_a- and E_b-curves which have the same numerical value, the relevant numerical value getting lower and lower as we move from the North-West to the South-East down the K-K' curve (see page 85 above). At each point on the K-K' curve an E_a-curve cuts the equally valued E_b-curve, both curves sloping negatively but the E_a-curve having the gentler slope. Let us consider any E_a-curve which cuts the contract curve (say E_{a1} at J) and any higher-numbered E_b-curve which cuts the contract curve (say E_{b6} at C). These two trade-expenditure curves will cut each other because the E_{a1}-curve will slope up to the left from J and the E_{b6}-curve will slope down to the right from C, both remaining South-West of K-K'. Moreover, they will only cut at one point (at E) because wherever they cut the E_a-curve, being lower-numbered, will have a gentler slope than the E_b-curve.

But consider an E_a-curve which cuts the K-K' curve (such as E_{a6} at C) and a lower-numbered E_b-curve which cuts the contract curve (such as E_{b1} at J). These also will certainly cut each other because the E_b-curve will move up to the left from J and the E_a-curve down to the right from C, both remaining North-East of the contract curve. But in this case they may cut each other more than once as at H, G, and F, because it is now no longer ruled out that the E_a-curve may be less gently sloped than the E_b-curve at a point of intersection (compare point G).

We can now turn to the solution of the three problems enunciated above on page 102.

In Problem I we are given the *ad valorem* rates of import and export duties in both countries and the rate of exchange. We can, therefore, calculate the slope of the price lines α and β from the formulae

$$\beta = \epsilon(1 + e_a + i_b + e_a i_b)$$

$$\text{and } \alpha = \epsilon \frac{1}{(1 + e_b + i_a + e_b i_a)}$$

(see page 100). We proceed then in Figure XLVII to draw the A- and B-trade-expenditure curves which have these given values. These are marked as $E_{a\alpha}$ and $E_{b\beta}$ in Figure XLVII. Their point of intersection gives the trading point Q of Figure XLII. We then complete the rectangle QUQ′T by drawing UQ equal to $e_b \times$ QH and QT equal to $e_a \times$ RQ. We draw the exchange-rate line ϵ through Q′ at the given slope. This cuts the X-axis at G, and GO is the size of the deficit which was our unknown. The rest of Figure XLII can then readily be completed by drawing the lines α and β through Q.

In Problem II we are given the size of the deficit and the value of the foreign exchange rate, and also all the *ad valorem* rates of import and export tax except the rate of import duty in A. We are to discover what rate of import duty in A is necessary to maintain the balance-of-trade deficit at the given figure at the given rate of exchange and with all the other given elements of commercial policy. If the balance-of-trade deficit is given in terms of A's currency we know the point G in Figure XLVIII and we also know the slope of the ϵ-line, so that we can at once draw the ϵ-line. Since we know the *ad valorem* rates of export duty in A and B we can, from the ϵ-line on which the Q′ of Figure XLII must lie, derive a corresponding line on which Q must lie by taking any point Z on the ϵ-line, drawing ZZ′ so that $\dfrac{ZZ'}{Z'K} = e_b$ and drawing ZW′ so that $\dfrac{ZW'}{W'C} = e_a$. Then W is the Q-point which corresponds to the Q′-point Z. We also know the slope of the β-line from the formula $\beta = \epsilon(1 + e_a + i_b + e_a i_b)$ and we can therefore draw the B-trade-expenditure line with this value $(E_{b\beta})$. Where $E_{b\beta}$ cuts the locus of W we have the point Q. Through Q draw the line α which has the same slope as the A-trade-indifference curve which passes through Q, cutting the X-axis at E. Draw FG such that FG = QT, and then $\dfrac{EF}{FH}$ equals the *ad valorem* import duty required in A to keep the deficit down to GO. The rest of Figure XLII can now be constructed from Figure XLVIII by drawing in the β-line through Q.

Finally, in Problem III we know all the *ad valorem* rates of import and export duty in both countries and we know A's balance-of-trade deficit. Our problem is to find what rate of exchange will give equilibrium. Let us suppose that A's balance-of-trade deficit is given in terms of A's currency as GO. We start then from the point G in Figure XLIX. Through this point we can draw free trade offer curves O_a and O_b. But we must now modify these free trade offer curves by allowing for appropriate trade taxes by means of the procedure described on pages 68–71 above. The intersection of these tax-modified offer curves O_a' and O_b' gives the trading point Q in Figure XLIX. Complete the rectangle QUQ'T by drawing UQ equal to $e_b \times$ QH and QT equal to $e_a \times$ RQ. Join GQ' and this gives the exchange-rate line ϵ. The rest of Figure XLII can now be completed by drawing the α-line and β-line through Q.

The application of the procedure described on pages 68–71 above for the modification of the offer curves to allow for the import and export duties is, however, not quite straightforward in the case under examination. When the balance of trade is zero there is no *real* difference in applying a given rate of import tax or of export tax. But when the balance of trade is in deficit and exports are less than imports a 10 per cent tax on exports is clearly a different thing from a 10 per cent tax on imports. Suitably modified offer curves can, however, be drawn by the means illustrated in Figure L.

Draw A's free trade offer curve (O_a) through G. Consider any point W on it. Draw W'W parallel to OZ. We wish to know at what point between W' and W will be Q, the point of A's tax-modified offer curve which represents a given *ad valorem* rate of export duty and a given *ad valorem* rate of import duty. Choose any Q.

Draw the line QH. Then if Q were the correct point, OH will represent A's exports. Draw FG such that $\dfrac{FG}{OH}$ equals the given *ad valorem* rate of export duty; and draw the α-line through Q tangential to the A-trade-indifference curve through Q to cut the X-axis at E. Then $\dfrac{EF}{FH}$ measures the *ad valorem* rate of import duty which together with the *ad valorem* rate of export duty of $\dfrac{FG}{OH}$ would make Q a point on the required modified offer curve. If, however, $\dfrac{EF}{FH}$ is larger than the predetermined import tax then Q must move to the right along W'W. This will reduce $\dfrac{EF}{FH}$ for three reasons: (i) OH will become larger, so that with a given *ad valorem* rate of export duty FG will increase, i.e. F will move to the left; (ii) E will move to the right because Q moves to the right; and (iii) E will move to the right because α becomes steeper (no inferior goods). Thus EF becomes smaller and FH larger. Thus at every height of the line W'W, a point Q can be found on W'W which represents the point W modified for given rates of export tax and import tax in A. The locus of Q is the appropriate tax-modified offer curve for A (i.e. O'_a of Figure XLIX).

CHAPTER IX

The Trade-Indifference Map and Economic Welfare

THE foregoing chapters have merely outlined the way in which, on our simplifying assumptions, various acts of policy—either of commercial policy or of transfers in the balance of payments between the two countries— could be depicted geometrically. The student who so wishes can now use this technique for assessing the desirability of various types of economic policy. But for this purpose the trade-indifference curves must be used in one way or another to assess economic welfare.

Consider the trade quadrant XOY in Figure LI in which Q represents a trading point at which A is exporting OM of A-exportables and B is exporting ON of B-exportables. There are three possible types of criterion of economic welfare.

(1) *The Nationalist Criterion*

The welfare of A is increased by a policy which shifts the point Q in a northerly or westerly direction from a lower to a higher I_{ta}-curve. Similarly, B's welfare is increased by a southerly or easterly shift of Q on to a higher I_{tb}-curve.

(2) *The Cosmopolitan Criterion, disregarding the Distribution of Income*

The world income can be held to be maximized whenever the point Q lies on the contract curve K-K', since if Q lies off this curve it is always possible for the citizens of one country to be made better off without those in the other being made worse off. This was the type of consideration which we discussed in connection with Figures VI, VII, and VIII. By inspection of

Figure LI it can be seen that there is a lozenge-shaped area (shaded in the figure) enclosed by the A- and B-indifference curves which pass through Q within which both A and B are on a higher indifference curve. In our figure Q needs to move in a north-easterly direction in order that both A and B should in fact be better off. But if the point Q moves on to the curve K-K′, even though it be on to a point which is not enclosed in the shaded area, it will have moved from a point at which the citizens of one country could have been made better off without the citizens in the other being made worse off to a point at which this inefficiency is no longer present. In this sense the movement of Q on to K-K′ would mark an increase in world income.

(3) *The Cosmopolitan Criterion allowing for the Distribution of Income*

But in order to tell whether in fact the economic welfare of the world has increased when Q moves (even though the movement be towards K-K′), we have to consider whether the gains of those who have gained do in fact outweigh the losses of those who lose. This we can do only by assessing the welfare obtained in A from a given consumption and that of B from another consumption, so as to add the two welfares together. A scale of welfare for A has been placed on the left-hand side of Figure LI against A's trade-indifference curves, and for B on the right-hand side of Figure LI against B's trade-indifference curves. These scales have been so constructed as to represent fairly rapidly diminishing marginal utility for increases of real income. Equal proportionate increases in the amounts of A-exportables and B-exportables available for B's consumption cause much less than equal proportionate increases in the utility scale of the corresponding B-trade-indifference curves. We now have more or less circular contours of equal total world welfare, centring round the highest point, Q', on the curve K-K'. The contour numbered 24 is shown in the diagram; it is constructed by marking the points at which B's trade-indifference curve marked 10 cuts A's trade-indifference curve marked 14, at which B's trade-indifference curve marked 5 cuts A's trade-indifference curve marked 19, and so on. The object of world economic policy now is to move the point Q up these contours as near as possible to the point Q' which marks the summit of the mountain.

Draw the price line α through Q' and let it cut the X-axis at C. Then it would appear that world income could always be maximized by allowing free trade (which ensures that Q will be on K-K') and then paying a transfer from country B to country A equal to CO so as to equalize the marginal utility of income in the two countries and to move Q' to the highest point on K-K'. But it must not be forgotten that, as was pointed out in discussing the problem of decreasing costs in connection with Figure XVII, there may be more than one contract curve. It is essential first to obtain that industrial structure in both countries which will place them upon the best contract curve before the policy of free trade plus income transfers is adopted.

This solution to the problem of maximizing economic welfare is, of course, subject to all the assumptions which we have explained in Chapter I. Of these two are particularly relevant.

First, it must be remembered that we have throughout been assuming that there was a given production block in each country, i.e. that the total supply of the factors of production was given in each country. This may not be so. The raising of income taxes and the payment of income subsidies connected with the international transfers may disturb incentives and so affect the output of the two products in the two countries.

Second, by assuming that each country was made up of a number of citizens with identical tastes and factor endowments, we have assumed away the effects which changes in trade policy may have upon the domestic distribution of income between rich and poor citizens of the same country.

Our geometric analysis does not allow for such complications of our simple conclusions about the best method of maximizing world welfare. But, subject to such limitations, we should strive (i) to obtain an industrial structure which brings countries on to the highest contract curve, (ii) to promote the freedom of trade, and (iii) to arrange for direct international transfers of income from those to whom income means little to those to whom income means much.

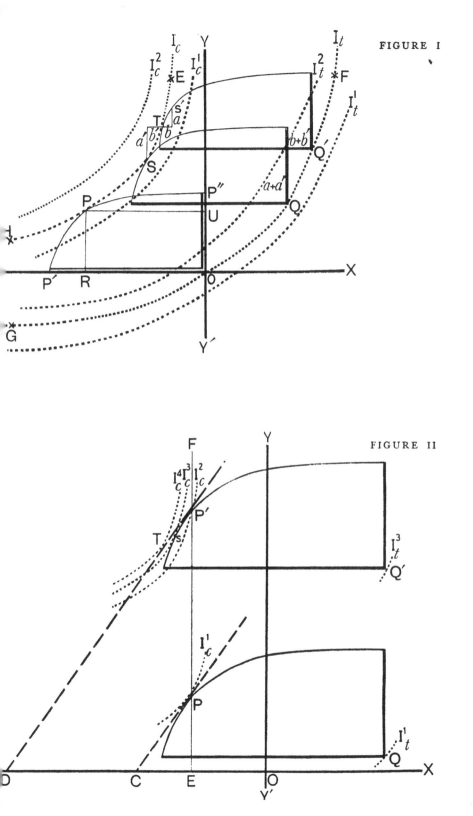

FIGURE I

FIGURE II

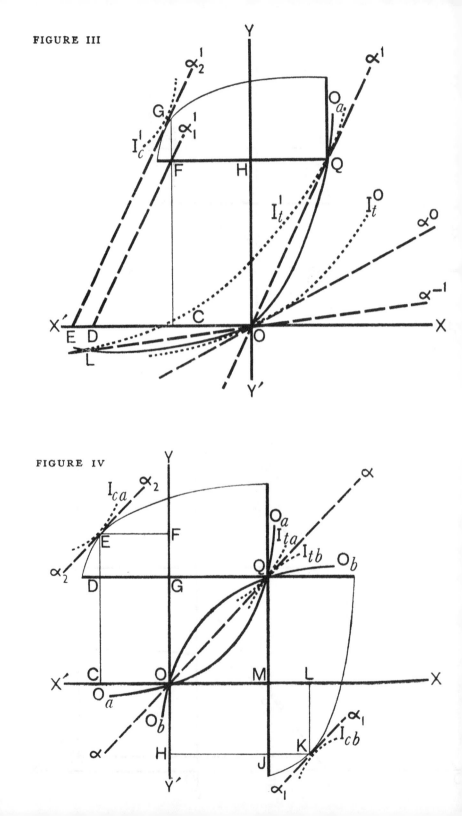

FIGURE III

FIGURE IV

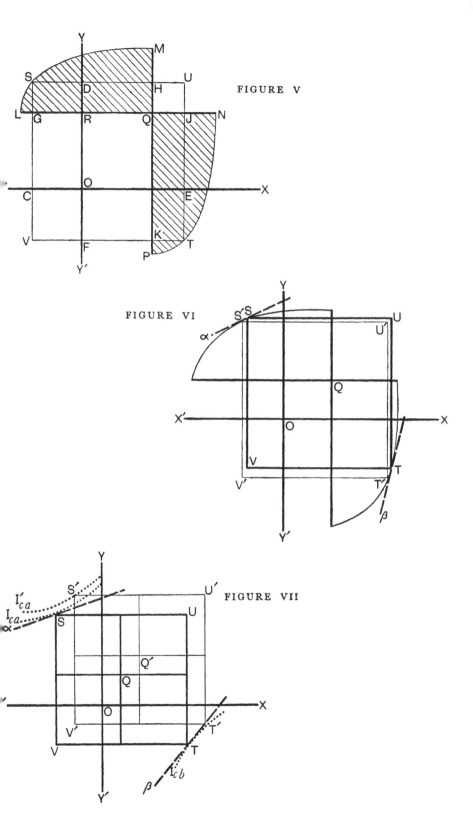

FIGURE V

FIGURE VI

FIGURE VII

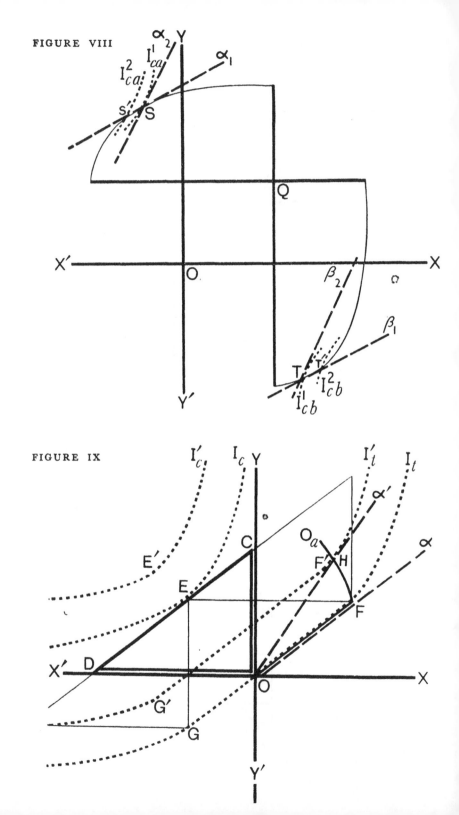

FIGURE VIII

FIGURE IX

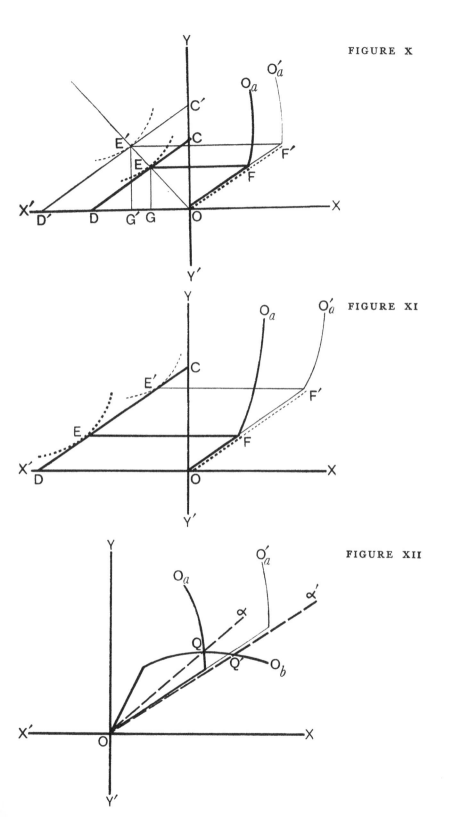

FIGURE X

FIGURE XI

FIGURE XII

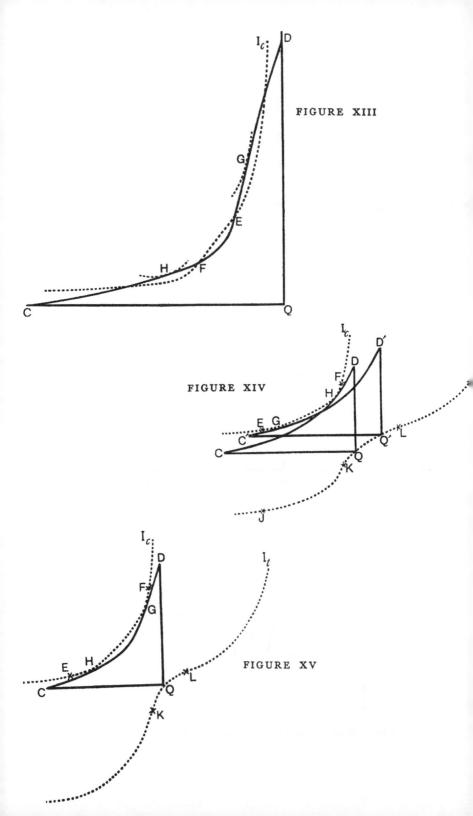

FIGURE XIII

FIGURE XIV

FIGURE XV

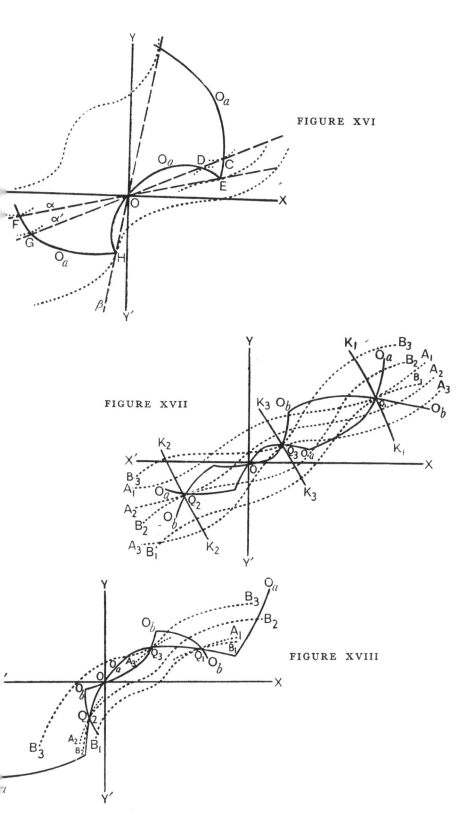

FIGURE XVI

FIGURE XVII

FIGURE XVIII

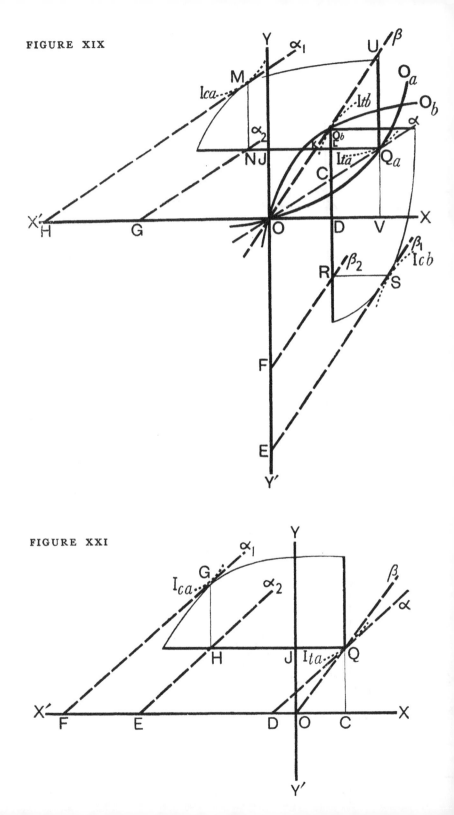

FIGURE XIX

FIGURE XXI

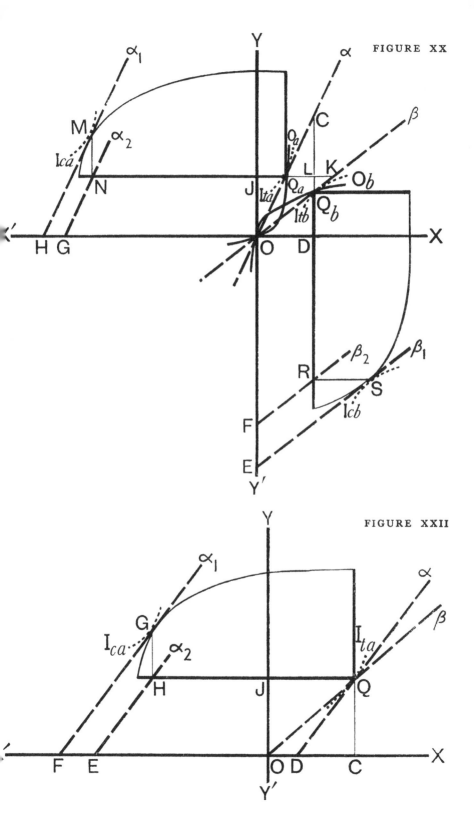

FIGURE XX

FIGURE XXII

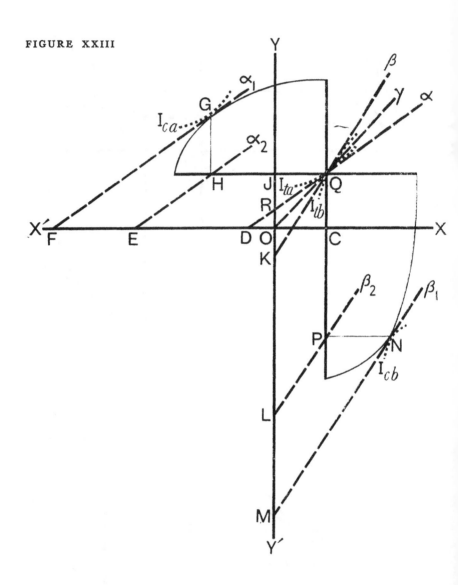

FIGURE XXIII

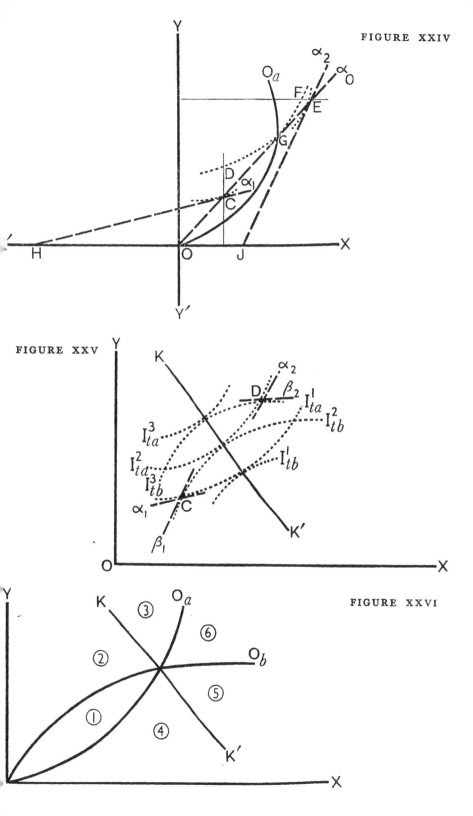

FIGURE XXIV

FIGURE XXV

FIGURE XXVI

FIGURE XXVII

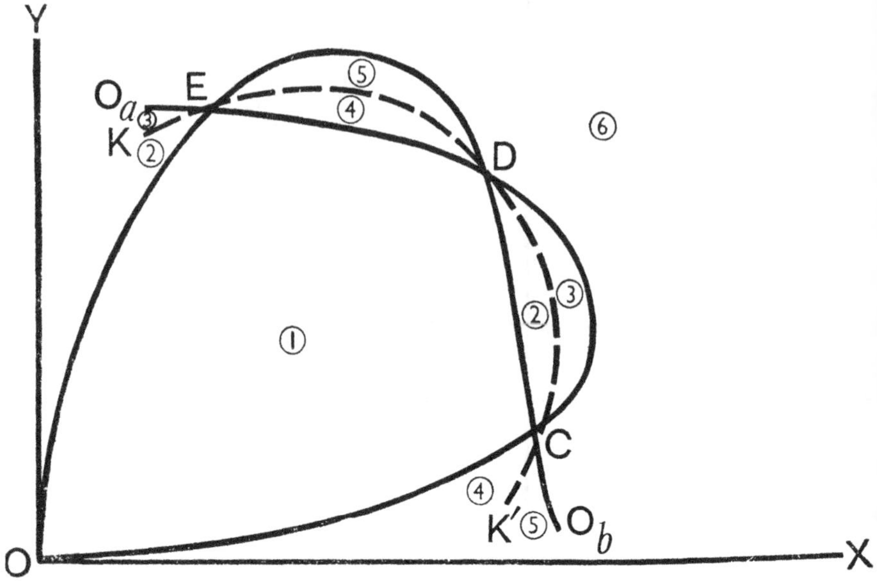

FIGURE XXVIII

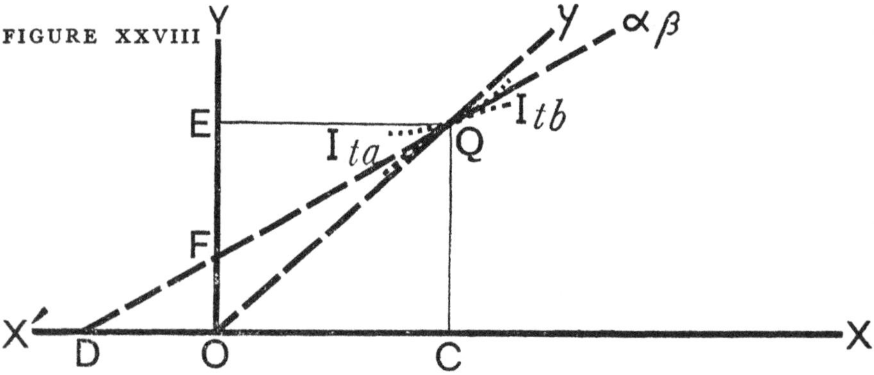

FIGURE XXIX

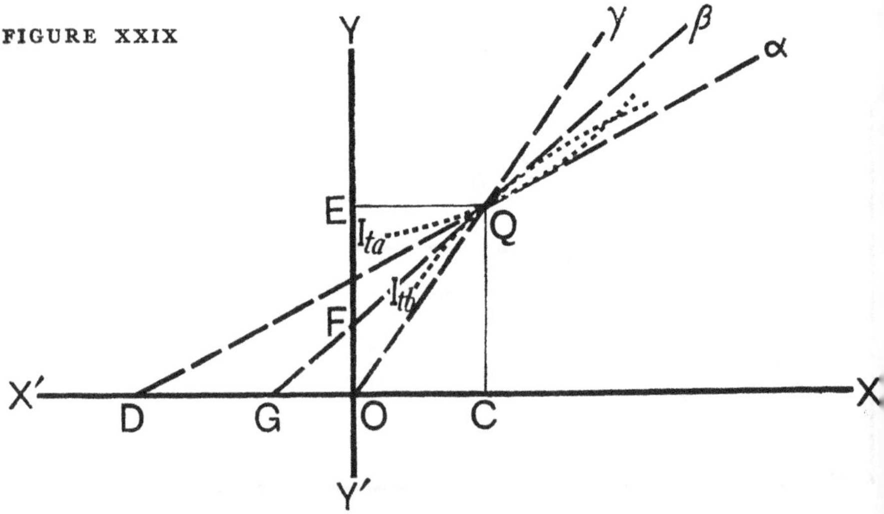

FIGURE **XXX**

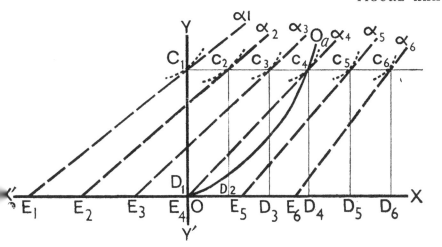

FIGURE **XXXI**

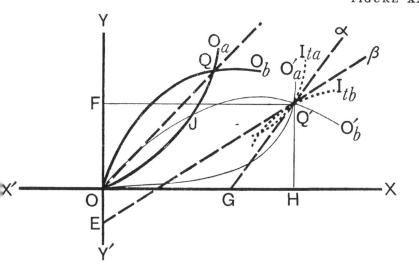

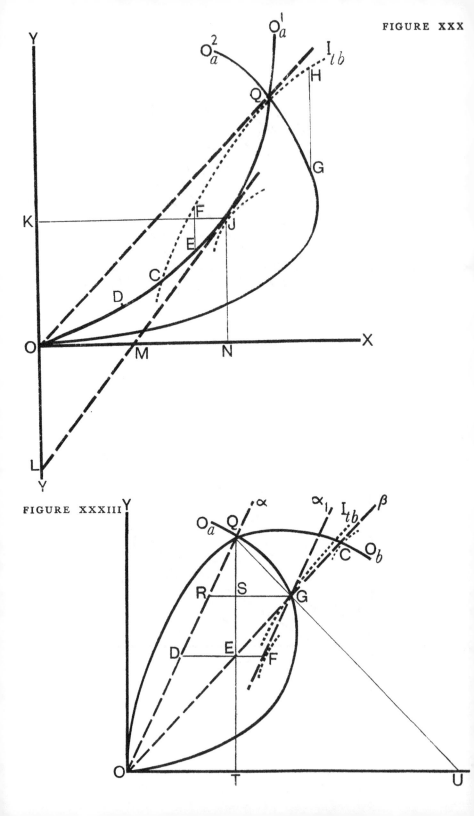

FIGURE XXX

FIGURE XXXIII

FIGURE XXXIV

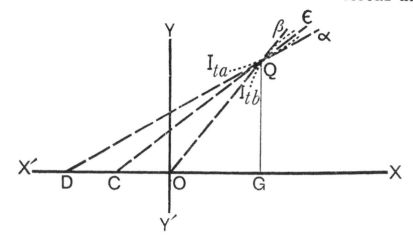

FIGURE XXXV

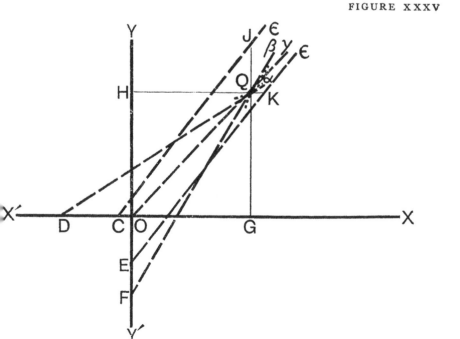

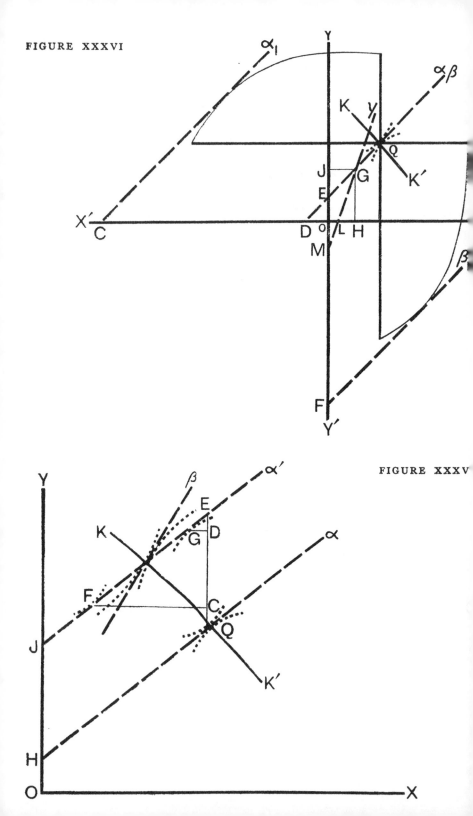

FIGURE XXXVI

FIGURE XXXV

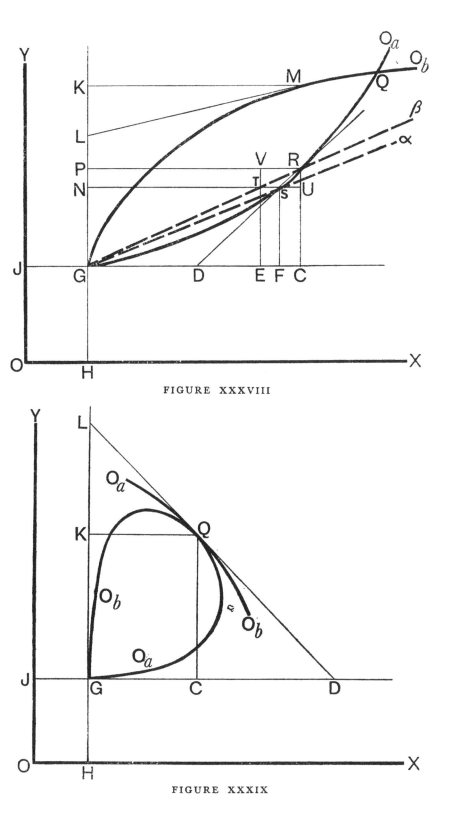

FIGURE XXXVIII

FIGURE XXXIX

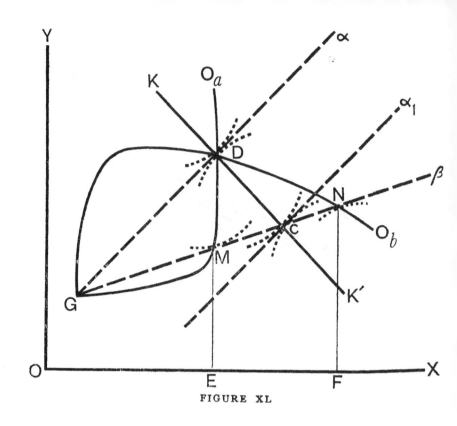

FIGURE XL

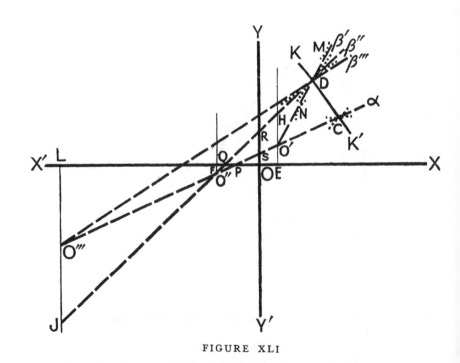

FIGURE XLI

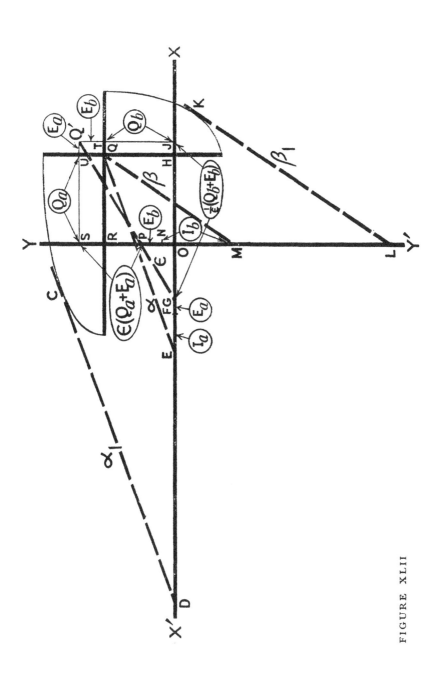

FIGURE XLII

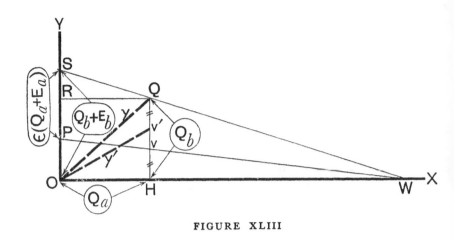

FIGURE XLIII

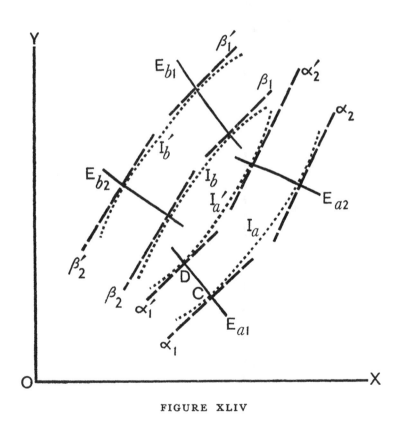

FIGURE XLIV

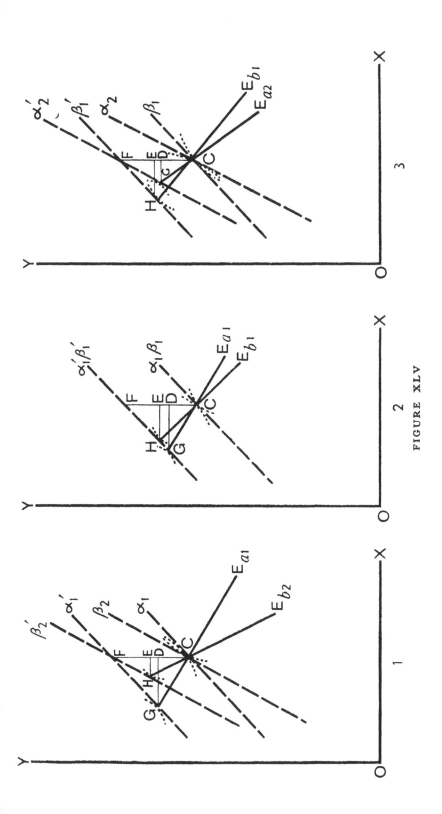

FIGURE XLV

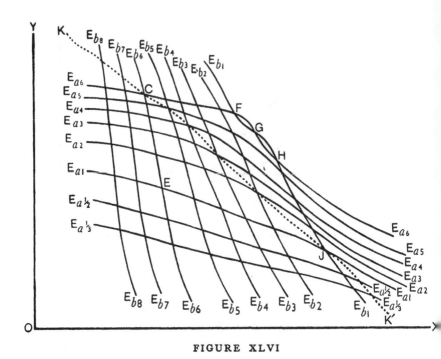

FIGURE XLVI

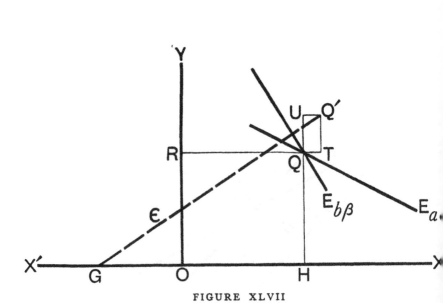

FIGURE XLVII

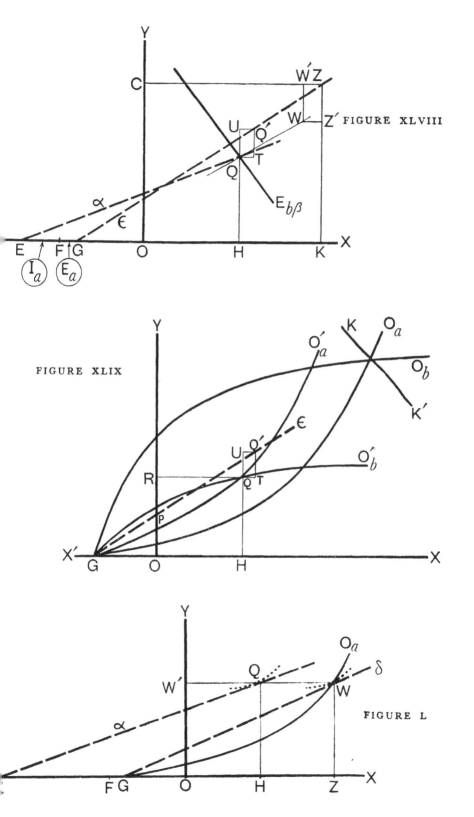

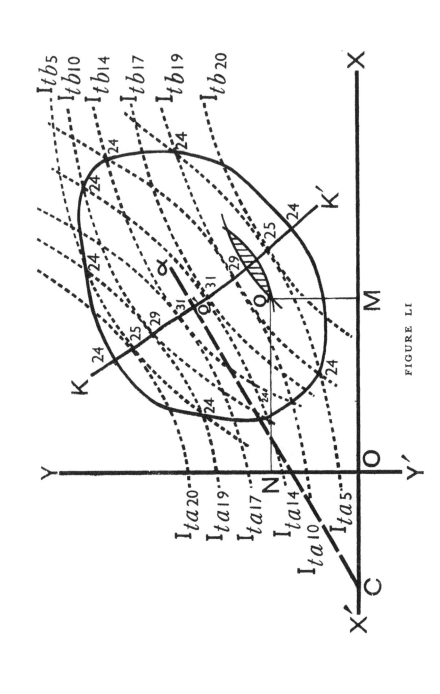

FIGURE LI

For Product Safety Concerns and Information please contact our EU
representative GPSR@taylorandfrancis.com Taylor & Francis Verlag GmbH,
Kaufingerstraße 24, 80331 München, Germany

Printed and bound by CPI Group (UK) Ltd, Croydon, CR0 4YY
08/05/2025
01864362-0002